Assessing the Impact of Computer-Based Instruction

A Review of Recent Research

Assessing the Impact of Computer-Based Instruction

A Review of Recent Research

M. D. Roblyer
W. H. Castine
F. J. King

The Haworth Press
New York • London

Assessing the Impact of Computer-Based Instruction: A Review of Recent Research has also been published as *Computers in the Schools*, Volume 5, Numbers 3/4 1988.

The Haworth Press, Inc., 12 West 32 Street, New York, NY 10001
EUROSPAN/Haworth, 3 Henrietta Street, London WC2E 8LU England

Library of Congress Cataloging-in-Publication Data

Roblyer, M. D.
    Assessing the impact of computer-based instruction.

    "Has also been published as computers in the schools, Volume 5, Numbers 3/4 1988" — T.p. verso.
    Includes bibliographical references.
    1. Computer-assisted instruction — United States. I. Castine, William H. II. King, F. J., 1927- . III. Title.
LB1028.5.R546   1988   371.3'9445   88-24377
ISBN 0-86656-893-X

DEDICATION

This volume is dedicated to the memory of
Servatius L. Roblyer

Father, by the light that from your window fell,
we see our task and
strive to keep your trust:
to labor well.

ABOUT THE AUTHORS

M. D. Roblyer holds a doctorate in Instructional Systems Design from the Florida State University. She has written extensively on instructional uses of computers and research findings in this area, and has developed a microcomputer-based package entitled *Grammar Problems for Practice* in conjunction with the Milliken Publishing Company. She is currently Professor of Computer Education and Co-Director of the Panhandle Center of Excellence in Mathematics, Science, Computers, and Technology at Florida A&M University in Tallahassee, Florida.

William H. Castine received the Ph. D. in Educational Research from the University of South Carolina in 1971. He is currently Professor and Chairperson of the Department of Secondary Education and Foundations at the Florida A&M University in Tallahassee, Florida, and teaches research methodology and educational measurement. He has been involved in numerous test development projects and has done extensive teacher training in instructional computing skills.

F. J. King received a doctorate in Educational Psychology at the University of Texas, Austin in 1960. He is Professor of Educational Research at the Florida State University where he teaches research methods, measurement, and statistical applications. Dr. King has been Project Evaluator on many instructional computing studies and development projects.

Assessing the Impact of Computer-Based Instruction

A Review of Recent Research

CONTENTS

ACKNOWLEDGEMENTS

Few activities voluntarily undertaken have more potential for temporarily ruining one's family, social, and professional life than writing a book. Between the moment that authors get the gleam of an idea for what will surely be their quintessential contribution to society and the golden day that final copy is dropped in the mail to the publisher, there is a twilight period when the spectre of the Unfinished Work overshadows all attempts at diversion or normality. Knowing that others have survived similar ordeals soothes but little. Thoughts of congratulations of family and friends seem too far in the dark future to be real. After a time, the authors recognize that the only thing which will really help is seeing the text bound and resting on the bookshelf.

For the authors of this review of instructional computing literature, this twilight period encompassed nearly two years, during which time the task of gathering and adequately summarizing research in this field assumed amoeba-like characteristics, growing and changing whenever the light fell on it. Just when we were sure we had included every important study in an area, someone would discover one more must-have item. A hundred decisions on what to include and how to include it were accompanied by several hundred calculations. Checking and re-checking led to still more calculations if an error was discovered. Sections were written and re-written as new information or a slightly better method of analysis was found.

Continual questions haunted these Sisyphean efforts: Do we have everything we should really have located? Have we found all errors we could reasonably have been expected to find? Have we addressed all issues which could realistically be included in a work of this kind?

The authors had the assistance of many people in escaping this gray labyrinth of never-ending computation and uncertainty. Our families supported us not only with sympathy and patience, but often with technical assistance, proofreading, and late-night runs to the library. We recognize here the unusual talents of Bill Wiencke, Kay Castine, Bill Castine, Jr., and Maxine King, as well as the continuing support of Becky and Tom Kelley. We also acknowledge the guidance and assistance of those family members who are with us now only in memory: Marjorie and Ray Wiencke and S. L. Roblyer.

We forgive with all our hearts the comments of our Tallahassee colleagues who made remaks like "Haven't you finished that *yet*?" and offer our sincere thanks to those who offered a positive contribution to the completion of our work. Especially appreciated was the assistance of Dr. Thomas Jackson, Dean of the College of Education at Florida A&M University. Judy Duffield's patient explanations to us on the "psychology of the Macintosh" were, we can acknowledge now, invaluable.

Other colleagues helped with words of encouragement and suggestions for additions or revisions. Among these, the names of Mr. Jack Roberts (Scholastic, Inc.), Dr. Gary Bitter (Arizona State University), Dr. Bill Bozeman (University of Central Florida), Dr. Sylvia Charp (*T. H. E. Journal*), and Dr. Harvey Long (IBM) stand out. They, themselves, of course, stand out as leaders in the field, and we consider ourselves fortunate indeed to have had their input to our work. We also thank those authors and researchers who took time out of hectic schedules to respond to our piteous cries for papers and reports to be sent *immediately*. Among these gracious individuals were Dr. Richard Clark (University of Southern California), Dr. James Kulik (University of Michigan), Dr. Terry Rosegrant (George Washington University), Dr. Diane Morehouse (Quality Evaluation and Development), Dr. Charles Blaschke (Education Turnkey Systems, Inc.), Dr. Henry J. Becker (Johns Hopkins University), Dr. Colette Daiute (Harvard University), Dr. Doug Clements (Kent State University), Dr. Gerald Gleason (University of Wisconsin-Milwaukee), Dr. Marianne D'Onofrio (Utah State University), Dr. Jill Gelormino (Florida State University), and Dr. Maureen Cheever (Northwestern University).

At the same time, we also acknowledge that some articles and reports which should have been included remain undiscovered, some errors have probably defied all our attempts at accuracy, and some important issues not discussed here will be pointed out by our readers in the months and years ahead. In some ways, these anticipated corrections and additions are part of the purpose for our undertaking this work. As Cleb Maddux points out in the Preface, science has taken a back seat to commercialism in the educational computing movement of the 1980's, and this machine must change directions if technology is to have any real impact on shaping an improved educational system for the future. If our publication results in bringing forth for public scrutiny research reports previously kept for local use only, if it instigates an outcry for further studies to reverse our tentative conclusions, if it acts as a springboard for increased discussion (however vehement) of the appropriate role of research in this field, we will have accomplished the most important goals of our work. If even one of these results from this book, then the months of tedium and neglect of our families will very nearly have been worth it.

M. D. Roblyer
Tallahassee, Florida
June 1988

List of Tables

List of Figures

Cleborne D. Maddux

PREFACE

This entire issue of *Computers in the Schools* is devoted to a research review authored by M. D. Roblyer, W. H. Castine, and F. J. King. It is with great ambivalence that I introduce this special issue. On the one hand, I believe this review of recent research on microcomputers in education marks an important and positive landmark in the evolution of our new educational subdiscipline. After all, the fact that there is now enough adequate research to justify such a review is a cause for rejoicing. Such was not the case only a few years ago, when research was scarce, and most published studies employed woefully inadequate designs and procedures. The fact that I am introducing the present study by Roblyer, Castine, and King is evidence that our field has made great strides.

On the other hand, this issue focuses attention on our problems and our shortcomings. It draws attention to what we know, and it makes devastatingly clear how much we do *not* know.

Perhaps it should not be surprising that a comprehensive review of research produces cause for both celebration and regret. It is the nature of science that inquiry produces more questions than answers, and no scientist worth his or her keep is ever completely satisfied with the state of the art in any discipline. Indeed, perhaps the greatest contribution of the Roblyer et al. review (and per-

---

CLEBORNE D. MADDUX - Associate Editor for Research, *Computers in the Schools* - is Associate Professor of Education, Center for Excellence in Education, Northern Arizona University, Flagstaff, AZ 86011.

1

haps the greatest contribution of any meta-analysis or other research review), is its tendency to stimulate readers to pause, assess past efforts, and formulate plans for the future.

Perhaps I was particularly susceptible to this influence, since I have been in a reflective mood ever since I wrote the research column for the last issue of *Computers in the Schools* (Maddux, 1987). In any case, the present special issue has caused me to cast an evaluative eye over the past ten years of developments in educational computing. Predictably, and in keeping with the ambivalent mood generated by the present review of educational computing research, I find both positive and negative developments characterizing our first decade of development.

The Hardware Shortage

As I mentioned in last issue's column, one of the most significant developments of the last few years is the widespread proliferation of computer hardware and software in education. There are approximately 2 million instructional microcomputers in America's public schools. Although more computers are obviously needed, the acute hardware shortage appears to be over. Hopefully, the field can now focus attention or research and on building excellent programs.

Educational Software

Another important development is the recent clear improvement in the quality of commercial instructional software. I have chosen to categorize educational software as *Type I* or *Type II* software (Maddux & Cummings, 1986). Type I software makes it easier or more efficient to use traditional teaching methods. Cognitively, user involvement is relatively passive, rote skills are emphasized, and control of the interaction between child and computer is largely predetermined by the software developer. Examples of Type I applications include tutorial and drill and practice software. Type II applications make new and better ways of teaching available and include word processing, simulations, and programming. (Roblyer, Castine, and King have found fascinating results in their review of research into these applications.) User involvement is relatively active, higher order thinking skills are emphasized, and control of the interaction between child and computer is largely in the hands of the child. Frequently, Type II software simply gives the child an empty screen and a powerful way to fill that screen with whatever the child desires.

Although both types of software are useful, I believe that the time and effort invested in computers can only be justified if teachers emphasize Type II applications. Unfortunately, Type I software is much easier to write, and in the past, the majority of educational software has fallen into this category. There does appear to be a trend, however, toward development of more and better Type II software.

Evaluating the Effectiveness of Software

We still have a long way to go, since excellent software of both Types remains scarce. However, there is now some significant momentum in the right direction. To maintain this momentum, however, practitioners must insist that software houses adequately research the effectiveness of both Type I and Type II products in educational settings. This will be a difficult challenge since producers of educational materials of all types have always been reluctant to subject their products to objective evaluation.

I am reminded of a 1972 study, in which researchers at the University of Arizona's Leadership Training Institute in Learning Disabilities asked 150 publishing companies to provide information about materials intended for use with learning disabled students (Kass, Lewis, DeRuiter, Schubert, & Archambault, 1972). These companies were asked to identify such materials and to provide results of efficacy research performed by their company. Each company was also asked if they were aware of research conducted by others using their materials. Responses were received from only 49 of the 150 companies, and many responses consisted only of a catalog of materials. The researchers concluded that very little research was conducted by publishers of special education materials, and that most publishers were unaware of research related to their products but conducted by others.

I suspect that similar results would be found if this study were replicated today with publishers of educational computing software. I see little evidence that many software houses are inclined to engage in evaluation research. More seriously yet, I also see little evidence that the field is inclined to demand that such research be carried out. A case in point is the recent proliferation of so-called *problem-solving software*. Such software has become extremely popular, and producers are making a great deal of money from its sale. Assumptions implicit in such software are that if students practice solving problems in the context of a computer simulation of an activity such as a detective solving a crime, problem solving skills will be improved, and these skills will transfer to other contexts.

The assumption of transferablility flies in the face of much of the existing research on problem solving in general. Linn (1985) has referred to this problem and points out that recent research by cognitive scientists has revealed that problem solving is much more discipline-specific than previously thought: "When students learn to solve physics problems, they learn about physics but not necessarily about problem solving in general" (p.15). She goes on to suggest that research has shown that when students learn to solve one type of problem they do not automatically or necessarily learn to solve other problems (p.15).

Thus, if software houses elect to market software that is not consistent with what is known about how people learn, the burden of proof that the software is efficacious should lie with the developer. Given the finding that transfer is not automatic, non-directed and unsupervised use of software such as *Where in the World is Carmen San Diego?* is not likely to result in improvement of general problem solving skills. There is, however, some evidence that certain teaching strategies can be successfully employed to promote transfer (Krasnor & Mitterer, 1984; Linn, 1985). Producers of problem solving software could profitably engage in research aimed at identifying and refining these strategies, and could then use the results to develop teaching manuals incorporating such strategies. A positive development related to this problem is the extensive research done by ETS on IBM's Writing to Read system. Roblyer, Castine, and King have included some particularly insightful comments concerning this landmark study. Although the efficacy study itself demonstrates a healthy trend toward proper evaluation studies of commercial materials, results of the study illustrate the dangers inherent in adopting materials that claim to be all things for all students.

In a related development, I have recently noticed what may be the beginning of an unfortunate trend for hardware and software developers to concentrate on development of materials intended to be self-contained instructional systems. I believe such ambitious developments are ill-advised if they minimize or eliminate teacher judgment by providing "canned" approaches and virtual scripts for teachers to follow.

Networking in Educational Settings

An example of the move toward canned approaches is the recent "hard sell" of various educational networking systems. Many of these systems cost tens of thousands of dollars, in return for which the supplier offers complete installation of all needed hardware and software. Software is usually installed on a hard disk system and management software is often included. I have addressed the advantages and disadvantages of such systems elsewhere (Henderson & Maddux, in press). A major problem related to software quality in networked environments is the fact that users are limited to use of software for which they, or the network vendor, can negotiate site licenses. This restricts the pool of software from which teachers may choose. This restriction may be unacceptable, since many software producers do not offer site licensing, and since it is difficult to find excellent educational software even when the pool of available software is unrestricted.

Other networking problems include determining responsibility for maintenance and repairs; ensuring that the management system provided makes use
of educationally sound principles of reinforcement, branching, etc. that are
also consistent with the philosophy and goals of school personnel; ensuring
that students do not erase commercial software or files stored by the teacher or
by classmates; providing for installation of new software on the hard disk, as
well as ensuring that such new software is compatible with the management
system; and making sure that needed inservice training is provided.

The Everest Syndrome

Although networking can be successfully implemented in educational settings, I fear that its increasing popularity is related to another trend that has
plagued educational computing since its inception. I have referred to this trend
as establishment of the *Everest Syndrome* in educational computing (Maddux,
1984). Those who have succumbed to this syndrome believe that computers
should be brought into educational settings simply *because they are there*. They
believe further that mere exposure to computers will be beneficial to students,
that computers ought to be used for any and all tasks for which software is
available or imaginable, and that, if schools can only obtain a sufficient quantity of hardware and software, quality will take care of itself.

The Overemphasis on Hardware

The result of the Everest Syndrome is an improper emphasis on computer
hardware, and a consequent underemphasis on other, frequently more powerful, variables affecting the computer user. In schools, this may result in computer implementations that over-emphasize what *hardware* can be *made* to do,
rather than what *children* using computers can be *empowered* to do.

The uncritical acceptance of educational networking is but one example of
the overemphasis on hardware. A second example is the disproportionately
large space devoted to hardware and peripherals in educational computing periodicals, compared to space devoted to other educational variables. Except for
the name on the cover, it is sometimes difficult to tell the difference between
periodicals intended for computer-using educators, and those intended for
computing hobbyists. Obviously, a preoccupation with hardware is appropriate in a publication designed for hobbyists, since such readers value hardware
for its own sake. Educators, on the other hand, supposedly value hardware in
precisely the same way they value books or typewriters - as teaching and learning tools.

The Undervaluing of Philosophy and Theory

Another manifestation of the Everest Syndrome may be the most serious of all. As a result of an inappropriate emphasis on hardware and what computers can be made to do, the importance of developing educational computing philosophy and theory is ignored or underemphasized. The evidence of our neglect of philosophy as it applies to educational computing lies in the absence of a significant body of discourse on what computers ought to be used for in education. Sidney Hook commented: "The only distinctive theme with which the philosophy of education has concerned itself from Plato to Dewey is: What should the aims or goals of education be?" (Hook, 1963, p. 51). Where is the literature debating what the aims or goals of computer education should be? Such literature exists, but it is extremely meager. Joseph Weizenbaum wrote an entire volume (Weizenbaum, 1976) centered on the question of what computers should (and should not) be used for in the culture at large, but litttle has been written on this topic specific to education. Of course, there has been extended debate about whether computers *can* successfully be used for one purpose or another. But that is not the same question as that to which I am referring. What has been neglected is work toward formation of an *axiology* of educational computing.

For example, there has been a strident debate centered around the use of Logo, and whether or not learning to program in this language can bring about a lowering of the boundary between child and adult thinking. But I have seen little, if anything, written concerning whether or not computers *ought* to be used for such a purpose. Until such issues are addressed, our progress will be limited, for we will have failed to agree on the proper relationship between human and computer in educational settings. In fact, in the absence of such a debate, we will even fail to specify our alternatives.

I continually encounter educators who have given little thought to such questions. For example, I was recently asked to serve on a committee of professors in my college who were proposing that the university fund a computer lab for graduate students in education. They had drawn up a plan and had even gone so far as to submit a proposed budget. When I looked over the plan, I noted that they were proposing that the lab incorporate a local area network. Since the plan also specified that the purpose of the lab would be for graduate students to write theses and dissertations using word processing software, and that all computers would be located in one room, I asked why a network was being proposed. I was told that the network would be used so that students could share information from machine to machine. When I asked why that would be desirable, and why students could not simply hand a hard copy or a diskette to the person they wished to share with, the committee members admitted that they had really given no thought to whether such sharing would be useful, nor whether the sharing of dissertation material was desirable from an ethical perspective.

The lack of consideration of philosophy leads to attitudes that might be characterized as *Everything Should Be Computerized.* In my opinion, this attitude has led to some clear computer abuses. Computers are not capable of human affect. Therefore, I believe that no task requiring human affective characteristics such as sympathy, empathy, and compassion should be turned over to computers. Yet software exists that is intended to analyze test scores, diagnose handicapping condition, identify special education placements, and write individualized educational programs for handicapped students. Computers can legitimately be used to streamline the rote aspects of the above tasks, such as typing of forms or conversion of raw scores to scale scores. However, the computer should not be used to substitute for clinical judgment or other exclusively human qualities.

Once philosophical issues are articulated, the next steps in the establishment of a discipline involve construction of theories, and then models. The clearest evidence that needed theoretical work has been neglected is when research in a field is of generally poor quality. Weizenbaum (1976) tells us that "One use of a theory, then, is that it prepares the conceptual categories within which the theoretician and the practitioner will ask his questions and design his experiments" (p.142). Poor theorizing necessarily leads to a neglect of research, or to poor research.

I am frequently struck by the extent to which professionals in educational computing resist attempts to focus attention on philosophical and theoretical issues. Nowhere is this more evident than in the host of textbooks now available for use in introductory teacher training courses in educational computing. Most of these books are not really books about educational computing at all. They are not about how to use computers as educational tools. They are, instead, books about how to *operate* computers using specific software. Thus, they teach teachers-in-training how to use word processing, data base management, and spreadsheets, for example, but they devote little, if any, space to why and how such applications should be taught to children. Another index of the atheoretical nature of many of these books, is the fact that many contain few, if any references, since the material is not based upon research or writing of others.

Roblyer and her colleagues have uncovered both encouraging and discouraging evidence related to this problem. The good news is that research on educational computing is increasing markedly, and the quality is improving considerably. Roblyer, Castine, and King review research conducted between 1980 and 1987, and three-fourths of the studies found were conducted between 1985 and 1987. The bad news is that while research quality is improving, much poor quality research continues to take place. One of the most striking findings of the meta-analysis presented in this special issue is that research into implementation of nearly all computer applications produces some positive and some negative results.

A Computer Myth

I believe this exposes a common myth about computers, and also says a great deal about the kinds of research that should be conducted in the future. The exposed myth is the common belief that all we need to do is place a computer and a child in the same room and wonderful things will happen. That is no more true for computers than it is for books. If it were true, all or nearly all findings would be positive. Obviously, there are other, more powerful variables than mere use of the computer. How the computer is used must constitute an important set of variables. Therefore, I believe that we need no more research intended to test computer vs. non-computer teaching. Future research should instead be aimed at finding the most effective ways of using computers at given grade levels, with given kinds of students, or in given subjects.

There is a parallel in my own field of special education that dates back to the 1960's. Researchers during that time conducted a series of studies that have come to be called the "efficacy studies." Such studies attempted to determine whether it was better to place special education students in segregated, special education classrooms, or whether it was better to place them in traditional programs. These studies failed for the same reasons that computer vs. non-computer studies are failing. Variables other than placement in a special vs. a traditional classroom determine success or failure for students. Then too, in special education, there was no such thing as one, or even several "traditional" or "special education" settings or sets of methods. Settings and methods varied more by individual teacher and school than by designation as traditional or special education. The question of which placement was better was not a sensible one. Neither is the question of whether math is best learned on or off a computer. Other considerations related to math teaching are more important, and should be the subject of research.

The Educational Computing Backlash

A final major problem is the fact that a backlash of public and professional opinion against educational computing continues to gather steam. This backlash has been fueled by the problems discussed above, but especially by the unrealistically extravagant and unsubstantiated claims that have been made by some educational computing advocates. As a result of these claims, there is a growing body of articles in both the popular and the professional press that is definitely *anti-educational* computing. I have been collecting these articles for approximately three years, and I currently have three thick file folders filled with them. This backlash threatens the future of educational computing. Innovations in education have been particularly prone to succumbing to such backlashes. Indeed, the *pendulum effect* is infamous in educational circles, and has led to the demise of nearly every electronic innovation of recent years. Examples include teaching machines, 16 millimeter film, and instructional television.

Logo Religionism

The problem of extravagant and unsubstantiated claims triggering a backlash is particularly evident with reference to use of the Logo programming language. Although I am a Logo advocate, I have frequently stated that I believe an unfortunate and unhealthy atmosphere of religionism has sprung up around the so-called *Logo movement*. Some advocates have become Logo true believers, and their advocacy seems based on mere testimonial evidence, or worse yet, on blind faith. As a cautious Logo advocate, I deeply regret the deification of the language, because I have seen other potentially useful educational movements abandoned as a result of such extremism.

The only hope of avoiding this fate for Logo is for advocates to tone down their claims, and for researchers to thoroughly and competently investigate the cognitive results of learning to program. I was tremendously encouraged by the Roblyer, Castine, and King findings related to research in this area. In keeping with my cautious optimism about the language, however, it should be pointed out that their findings are based on relatively few studies, and that they call for more research on this topic. I am becoming much more optimistic, however, that research can settle the controversy before Logo is abandoned due to disgust over its cult-like acceptance by extremists.

Conclusion

The decision to devote this entire special issue to a comprehensive review of research is based on my belief that thoughtful, rigorous research is our best hope for rectifying the problems mentioned above. I believe that educational computing is a tremendously promising field that is currently at risk. Roblyer, Castine, and King have done the field a great service by gathering together adequate research done over the past decade, and scientifically summarizing the results. Too few professionals have approached educational computing scientifically. Let us hope that Roblyer, Castine, and King are the pioneers of a new, objective tradition in our field.

PREFACE REFERENCES

Henderson, A., & Maddux, C. D. (in press). Problems and pitfalls of computer networking in educational settings. *Educational Technology.*

Hook, S. (1963). *Education for modern man.* New York: Alfred A. Knopf.

Kass, C. E., Lewis, R., DeRuiter, J., Schubert, M., & Archambault, E. (1972). Methods and materials in learning disabilities. In N.D. Bryant and C. E. Kass (Eds.). *Final report, Volume I, Leadership Training Institute in Learning Disabilities.* Washington, DC: U.S. Government Printing Office.

Krasnor, L. R., & Mitterer, J.O. (1984). Logo and the development of general problem-solving skills. *The Alberta Journal of Educational Research,* **30**(2), 133-144.

Linn, M.C. (1985, May). The cognitive consequences of programming in instruction in classrooms. *Educational Researcher,* **14**(5), 25-29.

Maddux, C. (1984). Breaking the Everest Syndrome in educational micro computing: An interview with Gregory Jackson and Judah L. Schwartz. *Computers in the Schools,* **1**(2), 37-48.

Maddux, C.D.. & Cummings, R.E. (1986). Educational computing at the crossroads: Type I or type II uses to predominate? *Educational Technology,* **26**(7), 34-38.

Weizenbaum, J. (1976). *Computer power and human reason.* New York: W. H. Freeman.

M. D. Roblyer
W. H. Castine
F. J. King

INTRODUCTION

The children of our society will never again know schools without computers. While technology's rapid evolution makes it difficult to predict its exact role in our future, the Computer Age has already had an irrevocable impact on our educational system. School offices, like business offices, have achieved greater efficiency through computerizing clerical and administrative functions. Teachers depend on computer tools to help relieve their paperwork burden. Students learn practical computer skills as preparation for college work and for life in a technological society. And, while there are no measures for this kind of impact, such benefits have earned computers a unique and permanent place in our educational system.

If the hundreds of articles written since 1980 are any indication, classroom instruction has also changed as a result of computer applications. Primarily because of the "microcomputer revolution," teachers appear to be more willing

M. D. ROBLYER - Professor of Computer Education and Co-Director of the Panhandle Center of Excellence, Florida A&M University, Tallahassee, FL 32307.

W. H. CASTINE - Professor and Department Chairperson, Secondary Education and Foundations, Florida A&M University, Tallahassee, FL 32307.

F. J. KING - Professor of Educational Research, Florida State University, Tallahassee, FL 32306.

11

than ever to consider using high technology in their teaching methods. The literature is rich with claims of unique effects for various computer-based methods, and some authors maintain that the new kinds of learning which computers make possible are actually changing the goals and curricular structure of education. The result: a new, more effective education for the citizens of a modern information society.

However, society currently has some very specific measures for the effectiveness of its educational system: student achievement, attitudes, dropout rate, learning time. After nearly 25 years of use in instruction, the impact of computer applications on these measures remains largely an unknown quantity. As educational decision-makers grapple with the fiscal demands of maintaining and expanding the instructional computing movement, they have urgent questions about the impact of computer-based instruction and other computer applications:

- Can computer applications help improve student performance in basic skills and other key areas?
- For what specific skill areas, grade levels, and content areas are computer applications most effective?
- Which kinds and levels of students seem to profit most from using computers to learn?
- Which kinds of computer applications are most effective for which skill and content areas?
- Can computer applications improve students' attitudes toward school, learning, and their abilities to learn?
- Will improved attitudes translate into better performance in school and lower dropout rates?

Although computers have been in use in instructional roles since the early 1960's, the answers to these questions remain largely unanswered--and the questions themselves are often unasked. Research results are ideally suited for addressing such issues, but educational decision-makers have rarely depended upon them in the past. Many factors are responsible for this casual attitude toward educational research (Roblyer & King, 1983), but up to now, lack of effectiveness data has not curbed educators' enthusiasm for microcomputers. Since their introduction in the late 1970's, microcomputer use in education has increased dramatically in spite of the lack of clear evidence of the contributions to teaching and learning. However, as we enter the second decade of microcomputer use, many educators are beginning to call for more equitable access to microcomputers for all students and for an expansion of the instructional role of computers in schools. The degree of financial and personnel resource commitment to accomplish this expansion would be so great--especially coming, as it does, at a time of declining resources for education--that it requires some objective information to justify the expense and effort.

While results of some research and evaluation projects are available, there are fewer than is desirable for answering the key questions on computer use, and most of them come from the pre-microcomputer era. From approximately 1965-1978, projects using large, mainframe-based systems produced research which seemed to indicate a promising future for computers as instructional delivery systems (Suppes & Morningstar, 1972; Lysiak, Wallace & Evans, 1976; Jones, 1978). However, computer use dropped off sharply after this time, and with it the research to yield specific information on how, when, and with whom computers should be used in education. Research projects to evaluate computer-based methods and materials are fewer in number now and, with some notable exceptions, are not as comprehensive as are needed in order to provide the answers which can guide teachers and administrators (Becker, 1987).

This discrepancy between widespread computer use and the small amount of research being done may be due in great part to the fact that the current movement was initiated and promoted primarily by K-12 teachers and students, rather than universities, as was the case in the 1960's and 1970's. Schools are not as likely to have the resources, expertise, nor the inclination to perform such research, since this is not normally their purview. Educational leaders at all levels acknowledge the necessity of increasing research in this field (Futrell, 1986) if we are to make any progress in determining the unique role of technology in improving educational quality. In the meantime, it seems essential that we listen to and apply the results of research that we have.

Rationale for Reviewing Instructional Computing Research

One study, even a very large, well-designed one, is made more useful if its results are examined in the context of others in the field. In light of the limited and unconcentrated nature of recent instructional computing research, it is even more important to gather and analyze the research which has been done. Through these reviews, we can not only ascertain if there are trends in findings which may guide development and classroom use of computers, we can also establish needs and promising directions for future research--a priority if the area is to continue its growth in a logical and productive way.

Several reviews of instructional computing research performed in the past few years have each yielded information to direct the course of computer use in education. The studies by Kulik and the University of Michigan staff (Kulik, 1981; Kulik, Bangert, & Williams, 1983; Kulik, Kulik, & Bangert-Drowns, 1985; Bangert-Drowns, Kulik, & Kulik, 1985; Kulik, Kulik, & Schwalb,

1986; Kulik & Kulik, 1987) focus primarily on meta-analyses and the implications of summary effect sizes. These findings provide useful, albeit global, information about the benefits of computers to various content areas and target groups. At the same time, such analyses have been roundly criticized for over-emphasizing the computer's role and not addressing the importance of other factors such as teacher intervention and software quality which can greatly influence the results of any given study (Clark, 1985). Meta-analysis reviews also rarely discuss important characteristics of the individual studies involved, concentrating instead on overall quantitative results.

Reviews by Kulik and Bangert-Drowns (1983-84), Hasselbring (1984), Roblyer (1985a), and Stennett (1985) are primarily "reviews of reviews." Like meta-analyses, these reports summarize results in a global way, rather than analyzing individual studies for methods and findings. Other reviews focus on special target populations (Orlansky, 1983; Crosby, 1983; Hasselbring, 1987), aspects of instructional computing implementation such as screen variables (Hathaway, 1984) or feedback (Carter, 1984), aspects of computer impact such as attitudes (Lawton & Gerschner, 1982), or certain content areas (Aiello & Wolfe, 1980; Burns & Bozeman, 1981; Roblyer & King, 1983; Willett, Yamashita, & Anderson, 1983; Okey, 1985) or types of applications (Hunter, 1987; Hawisher, 1986; Blume, 1984). Clearly, expanded reviews which discuss and compare study topics, methods, and findings, as well as analyze data, are also needed to supplement these more focused efforts.

The last comprehensive review of instructional computing research was that of Jamison, Suppes, and Welles in 1974. Of course, nearly 15 years ago, it was considerably easier to be comprehensive in this field. But even Kulik's meta-analyses published in 1986 and 1987 focus primarily on studies prior to 1980. Since that time, hardware, software, and classroom implementation have undergone dramatic changes. Microcomputer systems are often substantially faster (and occasionally slower) in presenting material and responding to student users than mainframe systems were. Certainly the logistics of microcomputer use are very different from those of mainframes. Too, instructional software on microcomputers often incorporates theories of teaching and learning which have come into common use only in the past five years. Many instructional techniques have actually gained recognition or experienced resurgence of interest through recent technological innovations themselves, e.g., Logo and discovery learning techniques. Applications such as word processing in composition writing have only recently been adopted to any extent. There is also a popularly-held belief that some current software is of higher quality than pre-microcomputer material because it reflects what we have learned over the years about how to make best use of the unique capabilities of the computer medium.

It is true that instructional computing with microcomputers is often more classroom-based than that with mainframes. Much inservice and pre-service training emphasis has been placed recently on integrating computer materials into teacher lesson plans and classroom activities (Roblyer & Castine, 1987). Because of this and because of the grassroots nature of the microcomputer movement, computer implementation seems more teacher-oriented than it was prior to microcomputers. There are usually more microcomputers available than there were computer terminals. In general, computer use in the 1980's takes place in a much different context from that of the pre-microcomputer era.

All these factors make microcomputer-based instructional computing a substantially different activity from what it was in 1974. However, to determine if these differences have resulted in improvements in achievement or attitudes of teachers and students, the evidence on this period in the evolution of computer-based instruction must be carefully reviewed and compared with what we have learned in the past. These comparisons will serve as a critical evaluation of how wisely educators have invested their time and resources in the microcomputer.

Scope of the Current Review

The purpose of this review is to provide as complete and up-to-date a picture as possible of trends in both research topics and findings, and of the contributions of instructional computing applications to educational effectiveness. The following will be covered:

1. *Summary of literature reviews and findings from 1975 to the present* - The methodologies of pre-1987 reviews are discussed and their findings summarized to provide baseline information for comparing recent methods and results.

2. *Meta-analysis of recent studies from 1980 to the present* - A small subset of the available instructional computing research contains sufficient data to include them in a meta-analysis. The results of a meta-analysis performed on these studies from 1980 to the present are reported, and this statistical technique is examined in light of recent criticisms of its usefulness. In addition, the studies included in the meta-analysis will be described, compared, and contrasted in order to identify trends in findings and reasons for the extreme variation in results from study to study.

3. *Review of findings from areas of interest* - This review places a special focus on major studies performed within the last few years which have yielded significantly useful--and sometimes controversial--results. Since word processing and Logo applications have generated intense interest in the field, this review devotes special attention to studies in these areas. It also describes results of studies on student attitudes toward school, subject areas, and themselves, and on student characteristics which seem to affect learning. Many

of these latter studies did not have suitable data to be included in a meta-analysis, but are still important to address in a review of recent research.

4. *Discussion of findings and implications for computer use and research* - Finally, the results of previous reviews are compared with current findings, and study methods and results are summarized for trends across areas. Perhaps most important, the findings of this review will be discussed in terms of their usefulness in answering the critical questions posed by educational decision-makers and in guiding the course of future research in this area.

FINDINGS FROM PAST REVIEWS

During the mid-1970's, funding for research and development in this area was at a level perhaps not to be seen again. Both researchers and funding agencies seemed captivated by the idea that computers could replace teachers in key instructional roles. In addition to numerous articles speculating on what computers could do to aid learning, no fewer than five reviews of research literature on instructional computing were done during the period between 1970 and 1980. (There may have been many more unpublished ones done by State departments and funding agencies.) However, the only review procedure available at that time was less than satisfactory. Reviewers had to (a) collect all the experimental and evaluation studies which compared a computer-based learning treatment with another instructional treatment (usually traditional classroom teacher-led instruction), (b) examine each study to determine whether or not it had found significant differences between the treatments, and (c) count up the number of studies which did and did not find such differences. This so-called "box score" method has frequently been criticized as yielding limited and subjective information (Slavin, 1984).

The box score method of summarizing results over studies was especially problematic for the instructional computing area, where differences in treatment effects were rarely large enough to reject the null hypothesis and most studies tended to show non-significant differences. In addition, although one could determine the number of studies yielding significant vs. non-significant (or negative) results, there was no statistical means of determining the practical significance of having a given number of studies in each category. It was difficult to get a meaningful picture of the usefulness of the computer-based treatments.

When Glass (1976, 1977) introduced meta-analysis as a method of calculating a more precise difference between experimental and control treatments, several reviewers of instructional computing research embraced this method wholeheartedly and compiled a number of meta-analyses in this area. Kulik's series of meta-analyses of instructional computing studies stands as the most thorough work of this kind, although other reviewers used this method on subsets of the studies he used (e.g., Roblyer & King, 1983, in reading and language computer-based studies).

The rationale behind meta-analysis is a simple one: to subtract the impact of the control or traditional method from that of the experimental method or the one under study and thus estimate the impact the new method would have over and above the old one. This estimate, known as the "effect size," is usually calculated by subtracting the mean score achieved by the non-treatment group from that achieved by the group of the treatment under study. The result is then divided by a measure of the spread of scores achieved by the two groups: the pooled standard deviation. This process is shown by the following general formula:

$$ES = \frac{\bar{X} - \bar{C}}{SD_P}$$

The effect size is stated in standard deviation units, a measure of the spread of the total population. An effect size of .25 derived from instructional computing studies would mean that the computer treatment raised performance .25 standard deviations over the other method in the study. Standard deviations can be converted to percentiles, a measure more familiar to and more easily interpreted by educators. An ES of .25 can be interpreted to mean that using the computer method results in average performance at about the 60th percentile, while students in the non-computer control group achieve on the average at about the 50th percentile. (See Figure 1.)

In an attempt to further define the impact of a given effect size, Cohen (1977) gives the following guidelines:

ES of .2 or less = small effect
ES of .5-.6   = medium effect
ES of .8 or more = large effect

While meta-analysis methods help to quantify the amount of effect due to a given treatment, they, too, have been criticized for what some researchers perceive as inappropriate applications and misleading results (Slavin, 1984). A discussion of specific problems is given in a later section of this booklet. It should be noted that meta-analysis, if used correctly, can yield useful kinds of information about instructional computing methods and products. However, as Kulik (1985) and others have noted, many experimental studies either do not report data required for calculating effect sizes or perform research in areas which do not lend themselves to producing such data (e.g., studies of attitudes toward computers). In these cases, box score methods, in combination with discussion of studies' methods and results, still seem the best way to summarize study results.

Since neither the box score nor the meta-analysis method has proven satis-

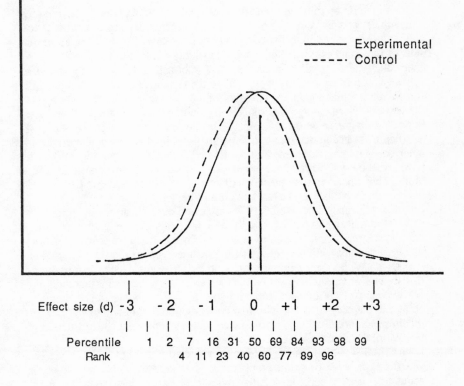

Figure 1.   Comparison of experimental and control
group distributions when ES = 0.25

factory for all review needs, both have continued to be used in several reviews of computer-based treatments in recent years. Although review methods have varied, the rationale has remained consistent: to examine the evidence on whether or not computer-mediated teaching approaches have any unique capability over other methods for improving the quality of teaching and learning. Some of the findings have also remained consistent over the years, regardless of review method. The following sections summarize the results of the individual reviews and the areas of apparent agreement and disagreement in their findings. The results of the reviews are also summarized in Table 1.

Previous Reviews of Effectiveness: Descriptive Methods

One of the first published reviews using the descriptive method was done by Vinsonhaler and Bass (1972) on ten studies of computer use in mathematics and language instruction. However, since they realized by looking at the results of these and previous studies that most had not found significant differences, they did a "modified meta-analysis," subtracting the average gain in the control group in each study from that of the treatment group. In almost all studies, they found advantages in favor of the computer group, and in most of the studies, this advantage was statistically significant. They found differences in gains were greater in the mathematics studies than in the language studies (3 to 10 months, as compared to 1 to 5 months). While they concluded that computer-based treatments seemed more effective in math than reading, they were tentative about widespread use of computer-based instruction for either discipline. They observed that questions of cost-effectiveness and comparative effectiveness with other media had yet to be addressed.

Jamison, Suppes, and Wells (1974) reviewed over 20 studies in computer-based methods as part of their overall review of "alternative instructional media." Other media considered as alternatives to traditional classroom instruction included instructional radio, instructional television, and programmed instruction. While their review took up over 60 pages of small print in the *Review of Educational Research*, Jamison et al. warn the reader that their survey is "relatively brief" and "inherently spotty" in its conclusions. They also point out that conclusions are limited to instruction within school settings and that information on costs is not included. Still, it represents the most comprehensive of the descriptive reviews.

One finding which was to be echoed repeatedly by subsequent reviewers was that a number of studies lacked adequate controls, were too flawed in some other way to consider in an analysis, or did not report data at all. Jamison et al. refer to the latter reports as "journalistic accounts," noting that it is "difficult to avoid feeling uneasy (about study conclusions) without supportive data." They did feel that such reports could still be useful to glean guidelines for evaluating more detailed reports which do provide data. However, because of the lack of quantitative information, the model proposed by Jamison et al. to assess the relative effectiveness of treatments by comparing the amount of input (e.g., time spent on each medium in the study) to the amount of output (achievement) was, by their own admission, difficult to implement.

In spite of the less-than-ideal circumstances of the review (which, of course, also prevailed in subsequent reviews), Jamison et al. did make some tentative conclusions about the selection of computer-based instruction as an alternative to traditional instruction. They concluded that CAI is apparently effective as a supplement to classroom instruction for elementary and remedial students, and that it could be used "in some situations" to improve achievement scores for such students. For secondary and college levels, they found that CAI had been used effectively as a replacement for traditional instruction. However, like Vinsonhaler and Bass, they emphasized the need to consider other cost-related factors in future experiments.

At about the same time as Jamison et al. reported their results, Edwards, Norton, Taylor, Weiss, and Van Dusseldorp (1975) did a review which focused solely on computer-assisted instruction. Their procedure was a true box score method, but a very comprehensive one. They located some 30 studies and coded them for type of CAI, subject area, grade level, supplemental or replacement use, and results (+ for significant, = for equal achievement, and - for negative results). Their findings were similar to those of previous reviewers in that CAI was found to be more clearly effective at elementary levels, and supplemental uses seemed more effective than replacement uses overall. CAI seemed equally effective as other non-traditional methods such as individual tutoring and programmed instruction, and appeared to show promise as a means of saving learning time. However, no firm conclusions could be drawn about the superiority of any type of CAI nor of the effectiveness of computer-based methods with lower or higher ability students.

According to its title, Thomas' (1979) review focused on the use of computer-based methods in secondary schools, but studies also were included from both elementary school levels and the military. Achievement, attitude, time reduction, retention, and cost data were reviewed. However, the review was purely a descriptive one; no box score tables were used to summarize the 60+ studies referred to in the text of the article. Although Thomas concludes that "the studies reviewed paint a positive picture for computer assisted instruction" (p. 111), 36 of the 49 studies found achievement results equal to those of other methods. The only results which showed a clearcut advantage for computer-based methods were those in time reduction. Thomas also concludes that cost factors continue to be an important factor in the adoption of CAI, but that the figures on cost-effectiveness are misleading since low-cost microcomputers were just beginning to come into use in schools.

Table 1
Summary of Findings on Instructional Computing Reviews of Research (1972-1987)

REVIEW FOCUS	AUTHOR(S) AND YEAR	Overall Achiev.	Drill	Tutorial	Other type CAI	Supplement
Drill/practice	Vinsonhaler & Bass (1972)	+				
All CAI	Jamison, Suppes, & Wells (1974)	-				
All CAI	Edwards et al. (1975)				No type more effective	+
CAI, CMI, CAG, and CAT	Florida Department of Education (1980)	-				
Military	Orlansky (1983)	-				
Adults	Kulik, Kulik, and Schwalb (1986)	ES=.42				
College	Kulik, Kulik, and Cohen (1980)	ES=.25				
Secondary	Thomas (1979)	-				
	Kulik, Bangert, Williams (1983) (1983)	ES=.32				
	Bangert-Drowns, Kulik, & Kulik (1985)	ES=.40				
	Samson, Niemiec, Weinberg, & Walberg (1985)	ES=.32		+		+

FACTORS ADDRESSED IN FINDINGS							OVERALL COMMENTS
Replace-ment	Female students	Male students	Time Savings	Attitude (Learning)	Type Students	Content Area	
						+ (math)	Ten studies reviewed
			+		Favored slow learners		"Findings of 'no significant differences' dominate research findings"
−			+		Favored slow learners (drill)		As effective as other non-traditional methods like PI and individual tutoring
			+	+	Favored elementary		No significant differences in most studies
			+				No difference between CAI/CMI & other methods in most studies
			+	ES=.34			CMI & CEI tended to have higher ES, but CAI more consistent ES; published studies had higher ES
			+	ES=.18			Nearly 3/4 of effects small-to-trivial; higher ES when two different teachers taught groups
			+				CBE effective as other methods
			+	ES=.12 & .19			Published studies had higher ES
				ES=.39 & .09	+ with slow learners		Higher ES with more recent, shorter studies, and with those for low-aptitude, disadvantaged. (80% of studies in math/science)
					+ with slow learners		Higher ES with shorter, published studies, with disadvantaged, in studies with different teachers, non-randomized groups

Table 1 (continued)
Summary Findings on Instructional Computing Reviews of Research (1972-1987)

REVIEW FOCUS	AUTHOR(S) AND YEAR	Overall Achiev.	Drill	Tutorial	Other type CAI	Supplement
Elementary	Kulik, Kulik, and Bangert-Drowns (1985)	ES=.47 (CAI)				
	Niemiec & Walberg (1985) (Also published by Niemiec et al. in 1987)	ES=.47 (CAI)	+			
Students w/mild learning problems	Crosby (1983)	+				+
Special education	Hasselbring (1987)	+				
Science	Aiello & Wolfle (1980)	ES=.42				
	Willett, Yamashita, and Anderson (1983)	+			+ (simulations)	
	Okey (1985)	.82				+
Mathematics	Burns and Bozeman (1981)	ES=.45 & .32		+		
				+		
	Glass (1982)	ES=.42		+		
Reading/language	Roblyer and King (1983)	ES=.35 (corrected)		+		
Word processing	Hawisher (1986)			+		
Attitudes	Lawton & Gerschner (1982)					

| FACTORS ADDRESSED IN FINDINGS | | | | | | | OVERALL COMMENTS |
Replacement	Female students	Male students	Time Savings	Attitude (Learning)	Type Students	Content Area	
					+ with slow learners		Lower ES with CMI = .07, higher ES with published studies
					+ with slow learners		Lower ES with CMI = .03 Higher with younger students, boys, exceptional students
							CAI seemed effective; insufficient evidence on CMI
							Drill is effective to increase fluency under certain conditions
							Higher ES in non-randomized groups; similar ES for CAI & PSI
							ES for CAI = .01, for CMI =.05 ES for simulations = 1.45 (One study); ES for PSI = .60
							Higher ES with tutorial than drill (.45 & .34); highest ES with drill for higher achievers (.47); for tutorials with older students (.52), disadvan. (.57)
							Good effects on computation but equal to tutoring and lower than ITV
							Higher effects with smaller groups, longer treatments, non-drill CAI, random assignment
							Small effect on writing quality but good effects on attitudes
							Insufficient evidence to draw conclusions

The State of Florida (Florida Department of Education, 1980) did a review of research in preparation for developing an instructional computing plan for the State. The findings were broken down as to computer-assisted and computer-managed or testing applications. Results of this review indicate there is some advantage to using CAI at the elementary level. However, the discouraging finding of "no significant differences" is the most common one in this review, as it was for Jamison et al. and Thomas.

A 1983 review by Crosby concentrated on the effectiveness of instructional computing (both CAI and CMI) on students with mild learning problems. Seven studies were reviewed, as well as those included in reviews by Jamison et al. (1974) and Edwards et al. (1975). The most significant finding of this review was consistent with that of these previous reviews: computer instruction used as a supplement to regular instruction achieved superior results to that used to replace classroom instruction. Crosby noted that very little of the available research involved microcomputers, and that this could influence future findings. She also observed that insufficient evidence exists to make conclusions about the usefulness of CMI for this special target population.

A more recent study on computer use with mildly handicapped learners by Hasselbring (1987) focused not on whether or not computer applications could be effective, but on the kinds of skills and applications which seem to yield the most promising results. He found that:

- Drill and practice is an effective strategy for increasing fluency in both math and spelling skills primarily when (a) students have already acquired strategies for retrieving answers from memory, or (b) drill is used as a follow-up to adequate tutorial instruction.
- Reading decoding skills seem to be enhanced by drill, but little evidence exists on computer effects with other reading skills.
- Insufficient evidence exists on the impact of word processing use, and more research is needed in this area.
- Little evidence supports the commonly-held belief that Logo use is helpful in the development of problem-solving skills.
- Simulations may assist in teaching problem solving if they are used in the context of teaching methods which help students identify and use appropriate information to improve decision-making.

Orlansky (1983) reviewed some 48 studies where the same courses were given either by conventional or computer-based instruction for military training programs. While achievement was equal in most of the studies, time required to learn the material was reduced through CBI in all but four of them. The median student time saved was about 30%. Although Orlansky observes that these findings differ from those of Kulik, Bangert, and Williams (1983) in their first meta-analysis review of secondary school studies, they may not, in fact, be that discrepant. The findings of no significant differences and a savings in learning time are consistent with those of all previous box score reviews of school learning. If Orlansky had done a meta-analysis, he may have found an effect size similar to that of Kulik. To further equate the usefulness of the two findings, Orlansky attributes the differences between his findings and Kulik's to differences between school education and military training. In school education, he notes, students are in school for fixed periods of time, no matter how long it takes them to learn a topic. In job training situations, student learning of a given topic is more self-paced. The increased achievement in school education may, therefore, be an equal benefit to a savings in learning time in military training.

Previous Reviews of Effectiveness: Meta-analysis Methods

In 1981, Kulik presented a paper comparing the results of meta-analyses performed by himself and other early meta-analysis reviewers (Hartley, 1977; Smith, 1980; Cohen, 1981; Ebeling, 1981) on computer-based instruction, programmed instruction (PI), and tutoring. One of the first reviews to use the technique pioneered by Glass (1976, 1977), the focus was on studies in mathematics. However, Kulik's purpose was not primarily to study computer impact on mathematics but to demonstrate the usefulness of meta-analyses in studying and confirming the existence of aptitude-by-treatment interactions (ATI). Kulik first observed that the results on each method of instruction were quite consistent across reviewers, finding for example, that tutoring raised achievement in mathematics .60 standard deviation units over traditional instruction, and PI had an effect size of about .01. There was also consistent evidence across reviewers that published studies yielded significantly higher effect sizes than dissertations.

Comparing the self-paced methods with the primarily structured-drill approach in computer-based studies, Kulik found consistent evidence of a grade-by-achievement interaction. The self-paced methods seemed to result in higher effects at the college level than at the elementary level. Just the opposite results occurred with the structured drill methods, which yielded much higher effect sizes with elementary students. Results seem to indicate that older students profit more from tutorial instruction, which they can structure themselves. Elementary students appear to do better overall with drill-type instruction which is already structured for them. Kulik did not, however, present any evidence on an ATI with regard to gender.

The University of Michigan By-Grade Reviews

On the basis of these initial results, Kulik and his colleagues from the University of Michigan performed several more meta-analyses on computer-based studies from various grade levels. The first of these, published by Kulik, Kulik, and Cohen in 1981, focused on results from college level studies. One noteworthy finding regarding the meta-analysis procedure was that only about 10% of the studies on CAI effectiveness had data sufficient to include them in the meta-analysis calculations. This finding appears to be consistent throughout the reviews by Kulik and by others. The average effect size on achievement in the college-level studies which were included was found to be about .25. Effects on attitudes were also generally small (.18 to .24). Nearly three-quarters of the studies showed trivial to small effects (.10 to .30), and only one-quarter yielded a medium-to-large effect (.50 to .80).

When Kulik looked at some 13 different study characteristics of the college-level studies to determine if any of them correlated with higher effects, the only one which did was that of control for instructor effects. Studies which had a different teacher for the experimental and control groups tended to obtain higher results. Kulik observed that the most significant finding across studies was on time reduction. In every study in which computer-based instruction was used instead of conventional teaching, students took less time to complete instruction--on the average of two-thirds less time. In spite of this promising finding, Kulik et al. concluded the "overall accomplishment of CBI at the college level must be considered modest," especially in comparison with other alternative methods such as peer tutoring.

The University of Michigan team performed two reviews of studies at the secondary level (Kulik, Bangert, and Williams, 1983; Bangert-Drowns, Kulik, and Kulik, 1985). Both of these found approximately the same effect size in achievement (.32 and .26, respectively) and attitudes (especially attitudes toward computers). However, the second review used a subset of 42 of the 51 studies from the first review, and there were several differences in review strategies and findings. Unlike the first review, the second study found that higher effect sizes correlated significantly with three study characteristics. Higher achievement was found in more recent studies, shorter duration studies, and with low-aptitude, disadvantaged students. Also, the second review separated the studies into traditional CAI, management uses (CMI), and unstructured computer-enriched instruction (CEI) such as using simulations and teaching programming to aid learning of mathematics. Effect sizes were significantly higher with CAI and CMI (.36 and .40 respectively) than with CEI (.07).

Although Kulik et al. attributed the significantly higher effects in recent studies to improvements in the technology, they also noted that none of the studies in this review was on microcomputers. Also, they observed a finding characteristic of all meta-analysis reviews: there was great variation in effect sizes among studies. The low effect size for CEI studies seemed to refute predictions about the usefulness of teaching programming to enhance problem solving skills in other areas. Both teams concluded that overall findings appeared to be better at this level than at the college level.

Kulik, Kulik, and Bangert-Drowns (1985) also reviewed results from 32 studies at the elementary level. This effect size was the highest of the three grade levels (.47 overall), giving final confirmation to Kulik's original hypothesis that there is an ATI with respect to computer-based treatments at different grade levels. However, in the four studies on CMI uses, the effects were substantially lower at this level (.07) than at higher levels. There were no significant relationships between higher effect sizes and other study variables such as type of CAI or gender of students. Kulik et al. noted again the limitation that no microcomputer-based studies were included in this review.

A final grade-level review performed by the University of Michigan reviewers concerned 24 studies with adult learners. Kulik, Kulik, and Schwalb (1986) included many of the studies used by Orlansky (1983) in his box-score review of computers in military training, but Kulik et al. also used several from non-military settings. Like Orlansky, Kulik et al. found that computer-based methods resulted in a substantial reduction in the amount of time required to learn given material. However, the two reviews reached different conclusions about the usefulness of computer-based treatments in increasing achievement. Orlansky found no evidence of any difference in effects on achievement between computer-based and traditional methods. And while, on the basis of Kulik's past meta-analysis findings by grade level, one may have hypothesized an effect size for adult studies lower than that found for the college level, just the opposite was found in the meta-analysis. An effect size of .42 was calculated on the adult learning studies, exactly that found in Kulik, Kulik, and Bangert-Drowns' (1985) review of elementary level studies. However, Kulik observed that a substantial portion of this effect size appeared to be due to the CMI and CEI studies, which had average effect sizes of .72 and 1.13, respectively. CAI studies had an average effect size of only .29, about equal to that found at the secondary level.

Two Final By-Grade Reviews

A report by Niemiec and Walberg (1985) on the results of a meta-analysis of elementary level studies was published at about the same time as that of Kulik, Kulik, and Bangert-Drowns (1985). (The same report was published again by Niemiec, Samson, Weinstein, and Walberg in 1987.) However, there were some fairly dramatic differences in methods and findings between the two reviews. While Kulik et al. reviewed 32 studies and concluded that there were no significant correlations between study characteristics and the size of effects, Niemiec and Walberg reviewed 43 studies (48 in the 1987 Niemiec et al. summary) and found evidence of several aptitude-by-treatment interactions (ATI). That is, they found that certain types of students seemed to profit more from CAI-based treatments than others. Specifically, the following groups had substantially higher achievement: Lower achievers, exceptional students, younger students, and boys. Tutorial CAI was also found to be more effective than drill applications.

Niemiec and Walberg mention mentally retarded, emotionally disturbed, and visually impaired groups as examples of the exceptional student population. It is not clear whether or not they mean to include gifted students, which are usually in this category, in which case their findings would be contradictory. Niemiec and Walberg also conclude that tutorial CAI was found to be significantly more effective than other forms of CAI, and that locally-developed materials resulted in better achievement than commercially-available materials. Several study characteristics also correlated with higher effects.

Several features in the review methods may help explain the differences in findings between these two reviews. First, Kulik may have had fewer studies than Niemiec and Walberg because the latter apparently included studies from Grades K-8. Kulik defined "elementary" as including only K-6. In addition, although the article version of the Niemiec and Walberg study is fairly brief and contains little description of meta-analysis methods, a paper presentation by Samson, Niemiec, Weinstein, and Walberg (1985) on secondary studies supplies more detail. The paper describes what may be a methodological error in the tests of significance. When calculating correlations between study variables and effects, each effect size in the review seemed to be considered an independent observation, regardless of whether or not it was one of several within a study. However, to obtain appropriate degrees of freedom for the tests of significance, one should consider all observations within a study as dependent and collapse them into one independent observation. The methods used by Niemiec and Walberg call into question their findings at the secondary level of aptitude-by-treatment interactions and of better results with tutorial, locally-developed software. If the same methods were used in their reviews of elementary studies, it also places limitations on how we may interpret their results at this level.

A Meta-analysis Comparing Computer-Based Instruction and Other Methods

In a report of a major study of CAI implementation in the Los Angeles Unified School District (Ragosta, Holland, & Jamison, 1982), Glass, the originator of the meta-analysis method, had a chapter describing the results of a meta-analysis of the study's results and comparing them with other methods: tutoring, Instructional Television (ITV), teacher training, and use of electronic calculators. Glass observed that the effects on mathematics achieved by tutoring and teacher training were about the same as those for CAI (ES = .43). ITV, however, yielded an effect size of from .53 to .86, with the effect increasing the longer ITV was used. The effects of the hand-held calculators ranged from a -.36 to +1.34, and Glass advised against averaging them. However, he felt there might be reason to believe that use of calculators was as effective as--and much less expensive than--CAI in increasing mathematics computation skills.

Reviews in the Content Areas

Another of the first published reviews to use the meta-analysis technique was done by Burns and Bozeman (1981) on some 40 studies of mathematics achievement. One of the most interesting findings was that studies using tutorial CAI seemed to yield slightly higher effect sizes overall (ES=.45) than those using drill and practice CAI (ES=.34). Although in most drill and practice studies, higher achieving students achieved about the same as disadvantaged students (ES=.32 in high achievers and .31 in disadvantaged), one study yielded a higher effect size for high/average students (ES=.47). With tutorial CAI, the disadvantaged students did substantially better than high achievers (ES=.57 in disadvantaged and .28 in high achievers). Elementary students seemed to do consistently better than secondary students in drill CAI (ES=.35 and .24, respectively) but less well than the older students in tutorial CAI (ES=.43 and .52, respectively). Boys did significantly better than girls (ES=.42 for boys and .17 for girls) in drill and practice studies. (No by-sex data were available from tutorial studies.) Since numbers of studies and effect sizes were relatively small, Burns and Bozeman caution against over-interpreting these results.

Aiello and Wolfle (1980), Willett, Yamashita, and Anderson (1983), and Okey (1985) all reviewed findings on studies of alternative methods of science instruction. The first of these reviewed 115 studies between 1961-1978 on five kinds of individualized instruction, including audio-tutorial (AT), personalized system of instruction (PSI), programmed instruction (PI), CAI, and combinations of these methods. The effect sizes calculated for CAI and PSI were among the highest (.42), surpassed only by the combination of approaches (ES=.47). Willett et al. also reviewed not only three kinds of computer treatments (CAI, CMI, and Computer Simulated Experiments or CSE), but also other instructional systems such as PSI and television/film. Of the 14 studies analyzed for the computer treatments, CSE was found to have the greatest effects (ES=1.45). Although this also proved to be the greatest effect size over all the other treatments, it represents findings from only one study and is, therefore, not a useful basis for drawing meaningful conclusions. CAI had an overall effect size of .01, while CMI had an effect size of .05. Mastery learning and PSI were found to have the next highest effect sizes (.64 and .60 respectively). In marked contrast to previous findings, a review of computer-based science instruction by Okey, performed in 1983 and reported in a 1985 publication, included only 12 studies, but found an effect size of .82.

It is not clear from the reports why Okey's findings differ so markedly from those of previous reviews. If one were to calculate a straight average of the effects found by Willett et al., the result would be an overall ES = .50. Okey apparently used different methods and/or studies to perform his meta-analysis.

In any case, this is clearly an example of where reporting *only* an average effect size from a meta-analysis would be misleading, since there is such a wide range of results. The best conclusion which could be drawn from this series of science reviews is that certain computer uses, e.g. simulations, offer promising results, while the majority of applications yield negligible benefits over other methods, and may actually be inferior to strategies such as PSI. Roblyer and King (1983) used meta-analysis to review the impact of computer-based treatments on reading and language achievement in 12 studies. An overall effect size, corrected for sample size, was found to be .35. Larger effects tended to be associated with studies which had smaller sample sizes, longer treatment periods, non-drill CAI, and random assignment to groups. The reviewers concluded that, although results are tentative, using computers in this area seems to be more effective when instruction is more individualized and supplemented with teacher help. Since using computers in this way means substantial increases in costs of instruction, it would probably be cost-effective to use computers in this area only if they were also being used for other purposes at the same time. It should be noted that no word processing studies were available to include in this meta-analysis.

Reviews of Non-CAI Computer Applications

The effectiveness of non-CAI computer tools has also been the subject of intense interest by many practitioners and some researchers. Blume (1984) summarized research from 16 studies on how instruction in computer programming (Programming Assisted Mathematics Instruction or PAMI) affected students' mathematical problem solving skills. He found that PAMI:

- Positively affects achievement for some mathematical content areas, but has negative or no effect on others. He observed that "PAMI's potential depends on its appropriateness for the content being studied."

- Can have a positive effect on problem solving if the programming activities are "tied directly to the solution of non-routine mathematical problems"
- Is more effective with junior high than senior high students

While Blume feels that there is some evidence to suggest that programming "contributes to improved problem solving because it promotes the development and use of a greater variety of problem solving heuristics" (p. 14), he concluded that current research is insufficient to provide clear support for this hypothesis. Part of the problem stems from the scattered nature of available research, with each study focusing on different problem solving variables and programming methods.

Hawisher (1986) reviewed some 24 studies of the effects of word processing (WP) use on writing skills. She, too, found that research reflected a variety of software packages, writing measures and variables, writing instruction methods supported by WP, and several different kinds of research methods. The case study method was used in nine of the studies. She concluded that:

- WP seems to enhance students' attitudes toward writing; students also feel positively about their WP use.
- Students showed increased attention to correcting errors.
- Researchers indicated mixed results of WP effects on number of revisions; most revisions seemed of the "surface" type rather than "meaning" type.
- WP did not seem to improve overall quality of writing in the majority of studies.
- WP seems especially effective when used by basic writers.

Reviews of Non-Achievement Factors and Effects

While most reviewers of computer-based methods and materials are interested primarily in effects on achievement, a few have studied the impact on attitudes and have reviewed ways of developing materials to emphasize effects on student learning. Lawton and Gerschner (1982) described the findings of several studies on attitudes of students toward computerized instruction. No effect size or box score was calculated, but the reviewers concluded that "there is very little agreement on attitudes toward computerized instruction." The reviewers felt that the general low level of computer literacy at the time of the study was responsible for this lack of consensus.

Hathaway (1984) reviewed variables of screen display and how they affect learning in computer-based materials. Just eight studies were reviewed on six different topics. While the low number of studies and absence of replicability must make his conclusions tentative, Hathaway found that:

- Any prolonged use of CRT's for reading information must be accompanied by breaks every 2-3 hours to prevent eye and muscle fatigue.
- Faster reading times result from using double-spaced text rather than single-spaced, although CRT reading is slower overall than reading of print.
- Upper/lower case print seems preferable to all upper case letters.
- Letter size and viewing distance should be considered together to create a maximum of .007 radians for the displayed letters. This size insures readability and maximum amount of text on screen.
- Graphics-enhanced displays of information seem to facilitate speed and accuracy in interpreting displayed data, although color has no advantage over black-and-white.

Finally, Carter (1984) reviewed study findings on aspects of feedback and their implications for software development. Her conclusions were that:

- Feedback should serve primarily to provide information on correctness, rather than reinforce and motivate.
- With lower-level cognitive skills, feedback should be immediate. With higher cognitive level skills, delayed feedback often seems more effective. Both seem to be more effective when the knowledge of results and the correct answer are provided.
- The most effective schedule of feedback is given when errors are made. It may also be that students should choose whether or not they want feedback at a given time.

Summary of Observations from Past Reviews

Information from the 26 reviews of past computer-based methods is an important and useful basis for examining present and future applications of computers in education. First, it provides baseline data and perspectives from authorities in the field on the contributions, issues, and problems with computer-based instructional methods. As most of the reviewers themselves readily admit, conclusions from these reviews about the usefulness of computer applications must be viewed as tentative. The research available from this field is amazingly sketchy in light of the present and potential commitment of funds for instructional uses of technology. Still, the studies which are available may be examined for trends in findings and compared with future results. Secondly, the review procedures themselves may be analyzed to determine needed modifications and methods for future reviews.

Consistencies and Trends in Findings

Although methods and focuses varied considerably from review to review, several findings appeared consistent across the summaries. One of the main reasons that all reviews did not reach similar conclusions was that each emphasized different variables of interest as measures of effectiveness. However, few clear disagreements were found among review findings, and nearly all reviews seemed to yield evidence that computer-based treatments offered some benefits over other methods. Other trends in the data included the following:

1. *Reduction in learning time* - Eight reviews at various grade levels concluded that using computer-based treatments resulted in substantially decreased learning time. However, most of the studies which looked at this variable seemed to be at higher grade levels. Kulik (1985) found that the savings in time was an average of 32%.

2. *Attitudes* - Findings from the Florida Department of Education (1980) and the University of Michigan studies indicate that attitudes are positively affected by computer-based treatments, but effect sizes are higher for attitudes toward computers (ES=.62) than attitudes toward subject matter or school learning (average ES=.22). The overall impact of computer-based treatments in improving motivation toward learning seems to be very limited.

3. *Content area* - In their box score review, Vinsonhaler and Bass (1972) concluded that computer-based treatments were more effective in mathematics than in reading/language areas. However, the overall effect size calculated by Burns and Bozeman (1981) for mathematics was equivalent to that found by Roblyer and King (1983) in reading/language. There was a broad range of effect sizes among the three studies of science instruction. Since the studies included varied greatly from review to review, it is likely that this is responsible for the disparity. Overall, computer treatments in science did not seem as effective as other alternative methods, notably PSI.

4. *CAI type* - Although Burns and Bozeman (1981) (mathematics), Roblyer and King (1983) (reading and language) and Samson et al. (1985) (secondary level) provided some indication of better results with tutorials than drills, just the opposite results were found at the elementary level (Niemiec et al., 1985, and Burns and Bozeman, 1981) and no clear trends emerged from other reviews. This could indicate that drill works better with lower level skills found at lower grade levels while tutorials are required for higher level skills. It seems evident that the success of the type of CAI is dependent on many variables, including type of skill being taught and instructional strategy accompanying the CAI.

5. *Supplemental vs. replacement* - Edwards et al. (1975), Crosby (1983), and Okey (1985) all concluded that CAI was more effective as a supplement,

especially at lower grade levels, but the evidence of this still seems largely based on opinion and individual interpretation of review results. Kulik and Bangert-Drowns (1983-84) point out that total reliance on the computer as a replacement for the teacher does not seem a practical nor effective strategy for CBE use. While early hopes were high that computers could reduce the high costs of education by eliminating teacher positions, this hope is dwindling. It seems likely that the computer's role is destined to be a supplementary one.

6. *Ability level* - Six reviews at various grade levels found that slow learners and under-achievers seemed to make greater gains with computer-based methods than more able students. This should not be interpreted to mean that any given computer-based instructional system, when used with high ability and low ability learners, would result in greater achievement with slow learners. Many of the studies which yielded high effects with slow learners were of systems *designed for* this population. Again, Clark's (1985) observation of the software making a dramatic difference may be operating here, since a given instructional system is most effective when designed with the needs of a specific target population in mind.

7. *CAI, CMI, and CEI findings by grade level* - An early hypothesis which Kulik developed and confirmed in his series of meta-analyses by grade level was that computer-based methods are generally more effective at lower grade levels. In a recent review of studies on adult learning, Kulik, Kulik, and Schwalb (1986) supplemented these findings with a report that effectiveness of CMI seems to increase at higher grade levels, while CAI effects seem to decrease at higher levels. Table 2 summarizes his findings:

Table 2
Summary of Kulik's (1986) Findings

	CAI	CMI	CEI
Elementary	.47	.07	-
Secondary	.36	.40	.07
College	.26	.35	.23
Adult	.29	.72	1.13

In a paper summarizing the findings across his reviews, Kulik's (1985) other conclusions about the effects of computer-based treatments were consistent with those described here. In addition, he noted several study features which seemed to correlate with study outcomes in his and other reviews. Among these were:

- Shorter vs. longer studies - Results were greater in shorter studies (ES=.36) than longer ones (ES=.27).
- More recent vs. older studies - Effects were larger in more recent studies (.36 in comparison with .24 in older studies).
- Published vs. unpublished studies - Effect sizes were reported to be consistently higher in published studies (ES=.46) than unpublished ones (ES=.23).
- Different teacher vs. same teacher - Effects were reported to be larger when different teachers were in charge of both computer and non-computer groups (ES=.40) and smaller (ES=.24) when the same teacher was present in both.

It should be noted, however, that the differences in the first two of these are small (within .15 of a standard deviation of each other).

Comparison of Review Procedures

Three kinds of review procedures have evolved over the past 20 years for summarizing research, and all three are still being used in reviews of instructional computing studies. Although meta-analysis procedures were developed in 1976 and are being used by many reviewers (Kulik, 1981; Burns & Bozeman, 1981; Roblyer & King, 1983) some reviewers still choose to use the box score method (Orlansky, 1983), and others simply describe study findings as "journalistic accounts" (Lawton & Gerschner, 1982). Each review seems to yield useful information, but each method has also been criticized for limitations in reliability. While meta-analysis methods would seem to yield the most quantitative information, some researchers feel its procedures incorporate assumptions which can lead to incorrect conclusions. (See discussion in *Meta-analysis Issues and Procedures* section.)

Certainly meta-analysis is of limited usefulness in summarizing research on attitudes (where few studies use control group findings as a comparison), where differing methods make great differences in effects (as in science findings), or on aspects of software which could maximize computer effectiveness (Hathaway, 1984; Carter, 1984). Also, while early reviews seemed more concerned with comparing computer-based methods with traditional methods, at least one researcher (Clark, 1985) contends that results from comparisons of CBE with traditional instruction are confounded by other factors such as teacher behaviors and instructional materials design. Meta-analyses have supplied us with useful information on trends in the data, but it seems clear that in the future, across-study effect sizes will not in themselves be a sufficient basis to draw meaningful conclusions about computer-based treatments. It seems important to supplement future comparisons of computer-based and conventional methods with examinations, both quantitative and qualitative, of the instructional conditions and target populations in which computer effects seem to be maximized.

These additional comparisons and focuses will not in themselves address all of the points Clark raises. In effect, he is saying that there is no point in doing further reviews or meta-analyses because "achievement gains attributed to the computer mode of delivery are probably due instead to the instructional methods employed in their 'software.' These methods could probably be delivered by the teacher." On the contrary, however, many of the applications described in recent studies could not be implemented by a teacher, e.g. simulations, word processing. Even in the case of drill and practice which can be done by teachers, it can be argued that teachers do not always do what they could do simply because they have a human aversion for tedious and repetitive tasks. While there would probably be general agreement that computer-based treatments should not be evaluated in isolation from the characteristics and quality of their software nor the effectiveness of their implementation strategies, it is important to note that, at their best, computer-based methods can offer a delivery system which is not possible and/or practical to implement in any other way. Computers can do well-designed instructional tasks consistently and reliably, as well as uniquely, in some cases.

As more and better software and applications for computer capabilities emerge, the need for further reviews of instructional computing research seems more urgent than ever. While the computer in and of itself may not be responsible for achievement gains over traditional methods, the computer delivery system, including well-designed software, may indeed be the factor which makes a difference with some skills and for some kinds of students. Clark is correct in pointing out that researchers must concentrate on investigating relative costs and efficiency of CBE and traditional instruction. However, it may well be impossible to fulfill his criterion of controlling for instructional methods, since the computer may be able to do in an individualized way the instruction which teachers find it impractical to do in traditional settings. The point of this research should not be to make the computer instruction exactly identical to teacher instruction, but rather to determine whether the computer-based delivery system has inherent benefits over the teacher-based delivery system, for whatever reason. When viewed in this way, the computer may indeed be found to be responsible for making possible greater learning gains.

Implications of Past Findings for Further Reviews

As Roblyer (1985a) pointed out in a review of reviews performed between 1974-1985, the effect sizes found for computer-based treatments should be viewed in light of those achieved by other alternative teaching methods. Kulik and Bangert-Drowns (1983-84) compared findings on CBE with alternative methods such as programmed instruction and found that the record for CBE appears to be much better by comparison. However, as Glass (1982) and Bloom (1984) reported, other methods and technologies seem to yield higher effect sizes than most of those found for CBE. (See Table 3.) In light of Cohen's (1977) criteria for judging the practical significance of effect size, most of the effect sizes calculated for computer-based treatments are small. Since the findings will have implications for cost-effectiveness, future reviews should compare their results not only with past findings in instructional computing but also with those of other alternative treatments and strategies.

Unless there is a rapid increase in research to accompany computer implementation in education, future reviews will have to contend with the same problems as those of the past: few available studies and many studies with inadequate data and/or flaws which prevent their inclusion in a review. Also, since past reviews included almost no microcomputer studies, future reviews should emphasize this technology and compare it with findings from mainframe studies. Finally, there is a need to concentrate in more depth on the study characteristics associated with higher effect sizes. Meta-analysis results should be supplemented with descriptions of and comparisons between studies, with special attention to analyzing results of large-scale, successful studies. Separate meta-analyses should be done for different content areas and target groups. Conclusions, however tentative, should be drawn about the practical significance of findings and their implications concerning the usefulness of employing computers to teach certain skills and students.

Table 3
Summary of Effect Sizes from Various Non-traditional Instructional Methods
(From Glass, 1982 and Bloom, 1984)

Non-Traditional Method	Effect Size
Glass:	
Reducing class size	
From 25 to 20	.05
From 25 to 15	.15
From 25 to 10	.25
Tutoring:	
Replacement	.87
Supplement	.61
Randomized studies only	.58
(Supplement)	
With IQ and grade equated	.43
Instructional TV (As replacement):	
1 year	.53
2 years	.70
3 years	.86
Special teacher training:	
Good and Grouws	.50
Anderson, Evertson, Brophy	.90
Electronic calculators:	
Range of effects	-.36 to +1.34
Bloom: (Selected factors from Bloom's list)	
Tutorial instruction	2.00
Corrective feedback process	1.00
Student time-on-task	1.00
Improved reading/study skills	1.00
Graded homework	.80
Classroom morale	.60
Peer and cross-age tutoring	.40
Higher-order questioning	.30
Teacher expectancy	.30

META-ANALYSIS ISSUES
AND PROCEDURES

The early reviews of instructional computing research offered by researchers like Jamison, Suppes, and Wells (1974) and Edwards, Norton, Taylor, Weiss, and Van Dusseldorp (1975), while helpful in establishing broad trends in the field, were not of much assistance to educators trying to establish a case for using computers in some area of instruction. Summaries of "box score" reviews are given in terms of numbers of studies which do and do not find significant results. For example, a given review might find 15 studies in all, with 6 having significant results, 8 with non-significant results, and one finding negative results. Interpretations of these kinds of summaries are, by their very nature, imprecise, open to criticism, and difficult to compare in any meaningful way with other review findings. For this reason, most early reviewers could give only very general and tentative direction to educators based on their findings.

When meta-analysis procedures were introduced in the late 1970's, they seemed at first to be the best solution to problems of summarizing review results. Certainly, they became very popular among reviewers in the early 1980's, and were used to summarize research results of studies in many content areas and of many instructional methods, including instructional computing. Their popularity arises from the fact that they have been used to yield not only a number indicating the level of effect of an instructional treatment on learners, but also to identify what variables in the studies have contributed to the observed effects.

General Meta-analysis Procedures in the Past

There have been many variations on the basic meta-analysis procedures, depending on the data given. However, the following steps were usually accomplished:

Step 1: Set criteria for studies to be included - This first step assured that the results of the meta-analysis are meaningful and useful. The reviewer must determine the minimum standards of acceptability for a study both in terms of methodology and reporting of results. Many meta-analysts have, for example, required that the study had no flaws in methodology which could render the results uninterpretable or unreliable. In addition, certain kinds of data must have been calculated or be able to be calculated from those given. Finally, because an effect size is based on subtracting the results of the control group from that of an experimental treatment group, only studies whose research design has both a control group and an experimental group were included.

Step 2: Identify variables which contribute to effect size - It is a reality of behavioral research that a given treatment may yield different results in different situations. Therefore, the reviewer must try to determine what aspects of the way studies were implemented contributed to higher achievement. Reviewers may include factors which they hypothesize will make a difference, or may include variables which have been found to make a difference in previous reviews.

Step 3: Find studies meeting criteria - The researcher must locate all studies which fall under the general topic of interest, then determine which of them will be included in the meta-analysis. Normally, this weeding-out process eliminates half or three-quarters of the studies initially located.

Step 4: Calculate individual study effect sizes - One study may have two or more measures of achievement and/or attitude. It may also have divided the subjects in the study into sub-groups (e. g., male/female, high IQ/low IQ) to determine differences among them in effects of the treatment. An effect size was calculated for each measure and subgroup, and then a combined effect size for the study was usually calculated.

Step 5: Correct individual study effect sizes for sampling error - The number of subjects included in the study is one factor which causes estimates of effects to vary. Since the purpose of the research is to generalize from the study to the population at large, this variation due to sample size is considered a source of error. Therefore, this error is corrected through a statistical procedure to arrive at a better estimate of the effect size.

Step 6: Combine individual studies to determine overall effect size - In order to make a general estimate of the treatment's effect for all students in all situations, effect sizes for all studies are combined and one overall effect size is calculated through an appropriate statistical procedure. Effect sizes can be combined across subsets of the studies, e.g., all studies in mathematics, at the elementary level, or those which report data separately for males and females. This yields a measure of the overall effect of computer applications for certain content areas, grade levels, or types of students.

Step 7: Identify relationship of effect sizes to study variables - Once effect sizes were calculated for each study, the reviewer tried to determine which study characteristics, if any, had the general effect of making achievement or attitude higher. This was done by calculating product-moment correlations between the overall effect size and each variable being considered.

Problems and Issues with Meta-Analysis

Meta-analysis procedures have come a long way since they were initially introduced by Glass in 1977. Statistical formulas and procedures have been periodically modified in an effort to make effect sizes a truer estimate of the impact of given treatments. Despite these improvements and the more precise nature of effect sizes in comparison to box score summaries, some researchers have consistently disagreed with the rationale behind certain aspects of meta-analysis and have also been critical of the way in which it has been applied in the field. Issues surrounding the use of meta-analysis have been hotly debated in the past few years, and, although the outcome of these debates is not yet clear, they will probably have the effect of improving the usefulness of meta-analysis to behavioral researchers. Three kinds of problems have been discussed to date, some having to do with the way meta-analysis is applied, and others with how its results have been used in research.

Methodological Problems

Meta-analysis has found its most articulate critic in Robert Slavin (1984, 1986, 1987). Of particular concern to him is the way in which meta-analysis has been applied by researchers in the past. He observes that they tend to combine "apples and oranges," that is, combining studies which have very different variables of interest, measures, and/or study designs. For example, Slavin criticizes a review of studies on class size and achievement by Glass, Cahen, Smith, and Filbey (1982) in which they include tutoring studies as a "class size of one." The results, Slavin maintains, are heavily weighted by the large effect sizes from the tutoring studies, thus yielding misleading results on the effect on achievement of lowering class size. He also notes that, although there are statistical methods of correcting effect sizes when they are found to have been due in part to some study implementation variables, these procedures are rarely used. In his review of seven different meta-analyses in the literature, Slavin (1984) found "sources of bias serious enough, in my judgement, to call into question one or more major conclusions."

Slavin (1984) also criticizes the heavy reliance on meta-analysis results. He feels that effect sizes "are not and should not be seen as data in the usual sense; they are merely useful summaries of study findings that must themselves be carefully considered." He also fears that one potential side-effect of meta-analysis is that it may discourage further research, which, he says, might prevent the development of important contributions to an area.

A different kind of criticism of meta-analysis is leveled by Clark (1983, 1985) and is directed specifically at applications of this procedure to reviews of computer-based methods and uses of other technologies. Clark maintains that looking at effect sizes from such studies alone gives the incorrect impression that effects are due exclusively or primarily to the use of the computer. In fact, he says, evidence exists to confirm his hypothesis that "achievement gains attributed to the computer mode of delivery are probably due instead to the instructional methods employed in their software," methods which he feels could be delivered just as successfully by a teacher. "Computers," he observes, "make no more contribution to learning than the truck which delivers groceries to the market contributes to improved nutrition in the community."

While Clark's analogy is a vivid one, his complete discounting of the unique contribution of computers to a given study's effects is probably an overstatement. Certainly, Clark's observation that the computer's instructional methods can be duplicated by a teacher is one of the essential questions these studies are seeking to answer. One would have to admit three premises from the outset: that it would be, at minimum, difficult for a teacher to emulate the methods of much available software, especially simulations and complicated branching programs; that it would be impossible for a teacher to duplicate the methods of any software except in a one-to-one tutoring situation; and that tool software such as word processors presents obviously unique capabilities. However, Clark's point is well taken that other variables in the instructional situation must be taken into account when interpreting the results of a given study. Indeed, an important research issue in this field is identifying any factors which seem to maximize the effects of the computer-based delivery system.

In response to Clark's truck analogy, it might also be noted that sometimes the truck has a critical role to play in affecting nutrition. For example, if there is no truck to bring the food to the people in Ethiopia, they starve. In the same way, computers, like other media, often play a very important role in bringing instruction to students who would not otherwise get it, either because the teacher is not available or does not know how to deliver the instruction adequately.

Despite all these objections, even the most vehement critics of meta-analysis admit the potential benefit of this technique for combining research studies. To make best use of meta-analysis, it is apparent that reviewers must (a) apply the technique as rigorously and systematically as possible, correcting statistically for any observed sources of error, and taking care to calculate separate effect sizes for dissimilar variables, and (b) interpret the results with caution and supplement them with analyses of the variables common to all studies which yielded particularly high or low results. Since all research findings must be considered within the context of limitations in study methods and procedures, including these kinds of descriptions in the review report will help readers understand the limitations of the review and draw more valid conclusions about its results.

Meta-Analysis Procedures in This Study

Some of the procedures in this review differed from those of past reviews. Most of these differences were due to new practices which have been developed recently for calculating effect sizes and completing meta-analyses. The details of these differences in procedures are reviewed below.

Locating the Studies

Research studies to include in the current meta-analysis were located through several fairly traditional methods. First, several Dialog searches were done of the ERIC and *Dissertation Abstracts* data bases to locate studies which met the pre-set criteria. These criteria included statistical requirements like means and standard deviations, as well as necessary information on sample sizes. Design requirements included having a control group. Only studies available after 1980 were included, and primarily microcomputer studies were sought. Each study had to be free from severe problems with methodology which would render its results useless.

To perform the searches, general keywords and key phrases like "Computer-Assisted Instruction" and "research," as well as specific ones like "Logo" and "problem solving," were used in various combinations until the most desirable kinds of results were produced. Abstracts of likely titles were reviewed and copies of studies which seemed to have data on effectiveness were obtained. Second, a by-hand search of the 1980-1987 issues of popular instructional computing and research journals was performed, and copies of potentially useful articles were obtained. Third, the 1980-1987 proceedings and programs from research and technology conferences were reviewed, and the authors of several papers were contacted and asked for copies. Fourth, well-known authors of recent non-meta-analysis reviews of research were contacted for copies of unpublished reports they used. Finally, the bibliographies of the articles and reports were reviewed for further studies.

Approximately 200 complete reports were gathered and read through these efforts, although over half of this number had to be discarded due to insufficient data or methodological problems. Two dissertation studies had to be omitted because they turned out to be the same studies already obtained in published form! Of the total number, 38 studies and 44 dissertations were able to be included in the analyses. Tables 4 and 5 on achievement and Table 6 on attitudes document the characteristics of these studies.

Table 4
Descriptions and Results of Research Studies in Instructional Computing

Study Authors	Year	Description of Study Design and Focuses	Content Area	N
Waldron	1985	Computer graphics package use vs. regular paper drawings to teach three-dimensional visualization; pretest-posttest control group design (Instructor-designed test)	Engineering (Drawing)	T=26, C=23
Fortner,Shar, & Mayer	1986	Computer simulations vs. workbook modules; randomized posttest-only control group design (Instructor-designed tests)	Science	N=40, C=39
Moore et al.	1980	Interactive CAI simulations vs. non-interactive PI-like presentations; randomized pretest-posttest design (Measured by errors made by students during subsequent labs)	Chemistry	T=249, C=222
Wainwright	1985	CAI-drill vs. paper/pencil worksheets; randomized posttest-only control group design (Instructor-developed test of chemical equations, attitude)	Chemistry	T=48, C=53
Henderson	1985	Video-assisted CAI to supplement instruction vs. regular instruction; randomized pretest-posttest design (Experimenter-developed math tests)	Math	T=58, C=43
Ferrell	1986	Computer-delivered math curriculum vs. traditional classroom delivery system; non-randomized posttest-only control group design (ITBS math subtests)	Math	T=50, C=41
Carrier et al.	1985	Two kinds of graphics-enhanced CAI vs. no graphics CAI vs. worksheets; matched pairs, pretest-posttest design (Instructor developed paper-pencil tests)	Math	T=71, C=73
Hawley et al.	1986	CAI-supplemented instruction vs. regular textbook-oriented instruction; randomized pretest-posttest control group design (Canadian Test of Basic Skills)	Math	T=39, C=40
Leigh et al.	1984	CAI drill vs. mimeographed sheets; matched pairs pretest-posttest design (Instructor designed test)	Math	T=24, C=24
Berlin/White	1985	Computer simulations vs. manipulatives vs. combination of simulations & manipulatives; randomized pretest-posttest design (Locally-developed measures of pattern recognition & orientation)	Math	T1=38, T2=37 C=38
Kraus	1981	CAI game for addition practice vs. no additional practice; math & reading control for each other (Instructor tests)	Math	T=10, C= 9
Massey & Gelormino	1987	CAI supplemented instruction vs. regular instruction; matched pairs pretest-posttest control group design (Clements Number Concepts Test)	Math	T=33, C=33
Horton & Ryba	1986	Logo-supplemented instruction vs. regular school program; randomized pretest-posttest control group with volunteers (Raven's Progressive Matrices Test of pattern analysis)	Problem solving	T=8, C=8

Grade Level	Treatment Length	Type CAI	Random Assignm't	Control?	Same/diff Teacher	Pub./ Unpub.	Overall ES
College	Varying time over 3 wks.	Tool: Locally designed graphics pkg.	N	No	Same	P	0.36
College	1 hr. each for 3 modules	Simulations: CONDUIT, MECC	Y	No	Same	P (ERIC)	0.47
College	1 semester	Simulation: PLATO	Y	CAI	Different(?)	P	0.78
High school	3 wks.	Drill: COMpress General Chem.	By class	No	Different	P (ERIC)	-0.43
9	Varying times over 3 mons.	Video-tutorial: Locally developed	Y	No	Mixed	P	0.98
6	40 min/day for 1 school yr.	Tutorial & drill: SRA	By class	No	Same	P	0.48
4	10-15 min/day for 14 weeks	Drill: Locally developed	Y	No	Mixed	P	0.23
3, 5	10 min/day for 71 days	Drill: Milliken Math	Y	No	Same	U	0.38
3	20 min/day for 5 wks	Drill: Milliken Math	N	No	T&C from same classes	P	0.44
2, 4	Varying times over 3 wks.	Simulations: PLATO	Y	1-Yes 2-No	Mixed	P (ERIC)	0.35 0.23
2	T=64 minutes C=85 minutes	Drill game: Fish Chase	Y	CAI	Same	P	1.45
Pre-K	Varied session-lengths over 8 wks	Unstructured CAI: Locally developed pgm.	Y	Yes	Same	U	0.6
Jr.high	2 hrs/wk for 7 wks +4 hr.sessions	LOGO	Y	No	Same	P	0.36

Table 4 (continued)
Descriptions and Results of Research Studies in Instructional Computing

Study Authors	Year	Description of Study Design and Focuses	Content Area	N
Perkins/Bass	1984	CAI-supplemented critical thinking curriculum vs. regular instruction in critical thinking; non-equivalent control group design (Test of Cognitive Skills, Otis-Lennon Mental Ability Test, Critical Reading Test, Inference & Prediction Test, Word Analogy Test)	Problem solving, critical thinking	T=35 C=58, 83
Battista & Clements	1986	Logo programming vs. CAI problem solving software; randomized pretest-posttest control group design (Experimenter-designed problems to solve)	Prob.solving & math	T1=6,13, T2=6,13 C=5,13
Pea	1984	Logo instruction vs. no instruction in planning skills; pretest-posttest design (Various experimenter-designed measures of planning ability)	Planning skills	T=16, C=16
Rieber	1987	Logo programming-supplemented instruction vs. regular classroom instruction; non-random pretest-posttest control group design (Experimenter-designed tests: Piagetian problems & geometry)	Prob.solving & geometry	T=25, C=22
Clements & Gullo	1984	Logo programming vs. CAI instruction to measure effects on thinking strategies; randomized pretest-posttest design (Peabody Picture Vocabulary Test, Matching Familiar Figures Test, Torrance Test of Creative Thinking, McCarthy Screening Test)	Various thinking skills	T=9, C=9
Reimer	1985	Logo programming-supplemented instruction vs. regular instruction; randomized pretest-posttest control group design (Brigance readiness tests, Torrance creativity tests)	Thinking/number skills; creativity	T=8, C=8
Degelman et al.	1986	Logo programming vs. no additional instruction; matched pairs posttest-only design (Experimenter-designed rule-learning test)	Problem solving	T=8, C=7
Piel & Butler	1986	Unstructured computer activities vs. regular school program; non-random posttest-only control group design (Experimenter-designed Piagetian classification/conservation tests)	Developmental problem-solving tasks	T=23, C=21
Alessi et al.	1982-3	Tutorial CAI vs. no instruction in reading; randomized pretest-posttest design (Instructor-designed reading tests)	Reading	T=13, C=18
Millar & MacLeod	1984	CAI and computer tools to supplement reading and math vs. regular instruction; non-equivalent control group design (Canadian Test of Basic Skills, Test of Divergent Thinking)	Math Reading/vocab.	T=65, C=34
McDermott	1985	CAI and CMI-supplemented programs vs. regular instruction in basic skills; pretest-posttest design (SRA Achievement Test)	Math Reading Lang. arts	T=1975, C=1778 T=1255, C=1343 T=1292, C=1370
Saracho	1982	CAI-supplemented instruction vs. traditional practice methods; pretest-posttest design (CTBS math and reading subtests)	Reading Math	T=128, C=128 "
Lavin/Sanders	1983	CAI-supplemented instruction vs. no additional instruction; pretest-posttest control group design (Metropolitan Achievement Test)	Reading	T=242, C=267
Reid	1984	CAI-supplemented instructional program vs. regular program; pretest-posttest design (Metropolitan Achievement Tests)	Reading/ language	T=126, C=123

Grade Level	Treatment Length	Type CAI	Random Assignm't	Control?	Same/diff Teacher	Pub./ Unpub.	Overall ES
7	50 min/wk for 9 wks	Unstructured tools: Rocky's Boots, Snooper Troops, PDI Analogies	N	Both a CAI & non-CAI control	Different	U	0.075
4,6	Two 40 min. sesions/wk (42 sessions)	Logo & various commercial CAI pkgs.	Y	Yes	Same	P	PS = .47 Math=.16
3 and 5	#1:30 hrs/yr #2:15 hrs/6mos	Logo programming	N	No	Different	U	0.01
2	1 hr. per wk. for 12 wks.	Logo programming	N	No	Different	P	PS = .99 Geometry=.60
1	80 min/wk for 12 weeks	Logo programming	Y	CAI	Same	P	0.34
K	35-40 min. for 1 month	Logo programming	N	No	Same	P	Thinking/number: 0.48 Creativity=.84
K	1 period daily for 5 wks	Logo programming	Y	No	Same	P	1.37
Pre-K	6 hrs over unspecified period	Unstructured: Locally-devel-oped pgms.	N	Yes	Same	P	1.44
Adult (Prison)	T=20 hours	Tutorial: PLATO	Y	CAI	Same (?)	P	0.74
7-10	80 min/wk over school year	Mixed: MECC, Milliken, Sunburst	N	?	Different	U	Math=.25 Reading=.08
3-6	Varied over 2 years	Commercial CAI & Locally-developed CMI	Y	?	Different(?)	U	Math=.42 Reading=.37 Lang. Arts=.29
3-6 (Hispanic)	T=60 hours over 1 year	Drill: CCC	N	No	Different	P	Reading=-.11 Math=-.13
2-9 (Chapter 1)	30 min/day for 1 year	Drill: CCC	N	No	Different	P (ERIC)	0.49
1-6	120 min/wk for 17 wks	Drill: KRS (District pkg.)	By class	No	Different	U	1.00

Table 4 (continued)
Descriptions and Results of Research Studies in Instructional Computing

Study Authors	Year	Description of Study Design and Focuses	Content Area	N
Watkins/Abram	1985	CAI game-based practice in phonics vs. regular classroom practice; randomized pretest-posttest design (ITBS and the California Achievement Test)	Reading	53 and 50
Goodwin et al.	1986	Adult-assisted CAI vs. unassisted CAI vs. regular classroom reading readiness methods; randomized pretest-posttest control group design (Experimenter-designed reading readiness test)	Reading	T1=27,T2=26 C=24
Hawisher	1986	Word processing vs. paper/pencil writing; posttest-only control group design (Experimenter-designed measures of # of revisions and writing quality)	Writing	1. T=10,C=10 2. T=40,C=40(?)
Kurth	1987	Word processing vs. paper/pencil writing; randomized posttest-only control group design (Length of compositions, number and type of revisions)	Writing	T=14, C=14
Kerchner & Kistinger	1984	Word-processing-supplemented writing program vs. regular writing instruction; pretest-posttest design (Test of Written Language)	Writing	T=18, C=19
Morehouse et al.	1987	Computer-delivered curriculum vs. regular classroom instruction, Also word processing vs. paper/pencil writing; pretest-posttest control group designs for all studies (Stanford Achievement Tests and experimenter-designed wholistic measures of writing quality)	Writing Reading Listening Language Mathematics	T=232, C=259 T=26, C=50 " " "
Murphy & Appel	1984	CAI-supplemented Writing-to-Read curriculum vs. regular early language instruction; pretest-posttest design (Unspecified standardized reading tests, writing assessment instruments designed for the study)	Writing Reading	Approx. 3970 included in calculations
Schaeffer	1981	CAI practice in structural skills vs. CAI practice in semantic skills vs. no practice; randomized pretest-posttest design (Instructor-designed German language test)	German	T1=24, T2=24 C=24

Grade Level	Treatment Length	Type CAI	Random Assignm't	Control?	Same/diff Teacher	Pub./ Unpub.	Overall ES
1	3 sessions of 15 min.each over 12 wks.	Drill: The Reading Machine	Y	Yes	Mixed	P	0.36
Pre-school	3 - 20 min. sessions	Drill: Stickybear ABC, Alphabet Zoo	Y	Yes	Same	P	0.00
College	1 semester	Word processor (Unspecified)	Y	No	Same	P (ERIC)	-0.30
10-11	Two-60 min. sessions/wk for 12 wks	Word processing: Word Perfect	Y	No	Same	P	0.09
4-6 (LD)	7 mons	Word processor: Bank St. Writer	N	No	Different	P	0.57
5-10	15 mons(Varied)	Word process.	N	No	Different	U	0.25
5	15 mons(Varied)	All types of	N	No	Different	U	-0.31
5	15 mons(Varied)	software:	N	No	Different	U	-0.09
5	15 mons(Varied)	Commercially	N	No	Different	U	-0.19
5	15 mons(Varied)	available	N	No	Different	U	-0.29
K-1	Computer use time varied	Drill: IBM phonics and CMI software	School & classes	No	Different	U	0.38
K-1							0.18
College	1 semester	Drill (Unspecified)	Y	2 CAI,1 No	Same	P	1.36

Table 5
Descriptions and Results of Dissertation
Studies in Instructional Computing

Study Author	Year	Description of Study Design and Focuses	Content Area	N
Feldhausen	1986	Author developed microcomputer modules vs. study guides to prepare for U.S.History tests with short-term intensive studying; Pre-test/posttest control group design (SRA Achievement Tests and instructor-designed unit tests)	History	T=103,C=113
Kaczor	1986	Traditional text & class approach vs. this approach supplemented by CAI drill to teach background information on small engine repair in vocational class; non-equivalent control group design (Written instructor-made test over subject matter)	Small engine repairs	T=19, C=14
Mason	1984	Traditional instruction vs.CAI-supplemented instruction in basic math skills for Educable Mentally Retarded with learning disabilities; pretest-posttest experimental/control group design (Iowa Test of Basic Skills, WRAT, PIAT, project-developed math test	Math	T=114, C=80 8 experimental, 8 control groups
Millman	1984	CAI drill vs. paper/pencil drill to improve attention towards math, basic math skills, and attitudes towards math. Pretest-posttest experimental/control group design (Author-developed instruments for all posttest measures)	Math and attention span	T=19, C=20
Englebert	1983	CAI drill + supplementary tutorial instruction vs. supplementary tutorial instruction only; pretest-posttest experimental/control group design (California Achievement Tests)	Math	T=32, C=24
Hamby	1986	Lecture & worksheets vs. lecture & CAI; pretest-posttest experimental/control group design (Investigator-developed measures for ratio & proportion math, attitudes toward math)	Pharmacology math	T=32, C=32
Reid	1986	Laubach tutorial method vs. traditional course vs. traditional course supplemented with CAI to improve math achievement in Adult Basic Education course; non-equivalent control group design (Test of Adult Basic Education)	Math	T1=8,T2=12 C=10
Crawford	1984	Traditional classroom instruction vs. CAI-supplemented instruction for business math; pretest-posttest experimental/control group design (Teacher-made tests)	Business math, accounting	T=27, C=30
Davidson	1986	Traditional classroom instruction vs. CAI-supplemented instruction; pretest-posttest control design (Metropolitan Math Test)	Math	T=18, C=36
Dyarmett	1986	Classroom & textbook vs. same supplemented with CAI. Non-equivalent control group design (Textbook accounting test)	Accounting	T=39, C=51
* Miller	1984	Traditional drill vs. computer-based drill; compared this pgm. to non-computer Chapter I programs in 3 other schools. (Portland Achievement Levels Test)	Math	T=272, C=80
* Ash	1985	Traditional drill vs.instruction supplemented with CAI drill; Pre-computer cohorts compared with classes the following year who used computers (California Achievement Test)	Math	T=171, C=51 5 classes

Grade Level	Treatment Length	Type CAI	Random Assign't	Computer Control?	Same/diff Teacher	Achievement ES
9-12	Two 40-min. sessions within 2 wks	Drill (Designed by author)	By class (Ten classes)	N	Mixed	0.12
9-12	4 mons. (Variable times)	Drill questions on AAVIM text on sm.engines	N	N	Mixed	0.67
LD/EMH Various levels	40 min/wk over 2 yrs	Misc: Milliken math, Kid Tyme, MECC, others	N	N	Different	.99 overall Elem.=1.19 Sec. = .90
LD (Elem)	5-30 min. sessions in 4 wks.	Drill & CMI (The Math Machine)	N	N	Mixed	.22 (math)
SLD (9th)	20 min/wk for 15 wks	Drill (Developed by experimenter)	N	N	Different	.16
College	1 hr.	Tutorial (PLATO)	Y	N	Same	.29
Adult	3 hrs/wk for 8 wks	Drill (PLATO)	N	N	Different	.40
College	120 min/wk for 3 wks	Business tools (Micro Learningware	N	N	Same	-.75
9-12 Chapter 1 students	13 wks	Drill (Various micro software pkgs)	By class	N	Same	.18
9-12	6 wks	Drill (Southwestern Pub. software)	N	N	Different	.16
5-8 Chapter I students	28 wks	Drill/CMI on CCC system	N	N	Different	.29
5 Upper 50th %tile	40 min./wk for 28 wks	Drill Milliken math, SRA, Sunburst geometry, PLATO	N	N	?	Computation=-.16 Concepts = .99

Table 5 (continued)
Descriptions and Results of Dissertation
Studies in Instructional Computing

Study Author	Year	Description of Study Design and Focuses	Content Area	N
Darling	1986	Traditional classroom instruction vs. instruction supplemented with CAI drill; pretest-posttest experimental/control group design (Knoxville City Basic Math Skills Test)	Basic Math	T=17, C=19
Turner	1986	CAI with paired learners vs. individual CAI vs. regular curriculum; groups within treatments pretest-posttest control group design (CTBS)	Math	T1=103, T2=105 C=105
Meyer	1986	CAI with graphics vs. CAI with no graphics vs. regular instruction with no additional practice; nonequivalent control group design (Stanford Achievement Test, School Attitude Measure)	Math	T=29, C=33
Elliott	1985	CAI-presented instruction vs. no additional instruction Pretest-posttest control group design (The 3-R's Standardized Test)	Math, reading	T=96, C=95
Levy	1985	CAI-supplemented instruction vs. traditional instruction; nonequivalent control group design (Stanford Achievement Test)	Math, reading	T=293, C=288
Easterling	1982	CAI-supplemented instruction vs. traditional instruction in both reading and math; experimental math & experimental reading control for each other, also control group (California Achiev.Test)	Arithmetic, reading	T=21, 21 C=24
Williams	1985	CAI drills in reading & math vs. no additional drill. Also studied relationship of learning style elements with CAI achievement. Non-equivalent control group design; each group controls for other. (Iowa Test of Basic Skills math/reading subtests)	Math Reading	T=148, C=152 T=115, C=127
Todd	1986	CAI drills in reading & math vs. no additional drill. Non-equivalent control group design; each group controls for other. (Iowa Test of Basic Skills, Estes Attitude Survey)	Math, reading	T=123,C=119 T=119,C=123
Abram	1984	CAI drills in phonics & math vs. no additional drill. Math and reading groups control for each other. (Iowa Test of Basic Skills)	Math, phonics	53 and 50
Ojeda	1984	CAI-supported bilingual program vs. non-CAI-supported program Pretest-posttest control group design (California Achievement Test)	ESL English	T=209, C=74
Noda	1983	Dual-language CAI vs. individualized instruction vs. lecture style format; pretest-posttest design (California Achievement Test)	ESL English	T1=35, T2=34 C=32
Pivarnik	1985	Word-processing-assisted writing vs. traditional writing methods; Randomized posttest-only control group design (Wholistic scoring of essays, Cooperative English Test)	Writing	T=40, 13 C=36, 13
* Wetzel	1985	Word processing vs. regular writing methods to compare effects on quality of writing (Scored by blind wholistic measures of writing samples on two assignments)	Writing	T=95, C=93
Cheever	1985	Word processing vs. regular writing methods	Writing	T=25, C=25

Grade Level	Treatment Length	Type CAI	Random Assign't	Computer Control?	Same/diff Teacher	Achievement ES
4 (low achievers)	1&1/2 hrs for 12 wks	Drill (MECC and Supermath)	N	N	Different	.27
3-4	15 min/day for 15 wks	Drill (Milliken math & Pet Professor)	N	N	Same	Overall=.34 Boys=.29,.41 Girls=.33,.31
1-5 (low achievers)	20 min.3 times/wk 18 wks	Various kinds (Unspecified sources)	N	N	Different	Graphics=.49 Non-grap=.32
11-12	1 hr/wk for 1 semester	Tutorial (Micro-PLATO)	Y	N	Mixed	Reading=.00 Lang. =.71 Math =.20
5	20 min.3 times/wk,1yr	Drill (ISI system)	N	Y	Different	Reading=.30 Math = .21
5	30 min/wk for 16 wks	Drill (SRA math, MicroSystem 80)	Y	Y	Different	Reading=-.03 Math=.10
4	15 min/day for 7 mons.	Drill (Diascriptive reading & Milliken math)	N	Y	Different	Reading=-.31 Math = .17
4	15 min/day for 7 mons.	Drill Diascriptive Reading,Milliken	N	Y	Different	Reading=-.35 Math = .74
1	45 min/wk for 12 wks	Drill (The Reading Machine,The Math Machine)	Y	Y	Different	Reading=.28 Math =.24
6-12	1 hr/wk for 6 mons.	Tutorial/CMI (Developed by Detroit Public Schools)	N	N	Different	Overall=-.19 Boys =-.40 Girls= .03
6-8	100 min/wk for 6 mons.	Tutorial/CMI (Developed by Detroit PS)	N	N	?	vs.ctrl=.75 vs.indiv=.44
9-11 (below average)	-	WP (Wordstar)	Y	N	Same	Lang.= .29 Writing=.73
3-5	30 min/wk for 10 wks	WP (Bank Street Writer)	N	N	Different	-.10
4	40 min/wk for 1 school yr.	WP (Magic Slate)	N	N	Different	0.25

Table 5 (continued)
Descriptions and Results of Dissertation
Studies in Instructional Computing

Study Author	Year	Description of Study Design and Focuses	Content Area	N
Bryg	1984	CAI-supplemented reading instruction vs. traditional basal readers and curriculum; non-randomized pretest-posttest design (California Achievement Tests, Attitude Toward School Scale, Attitude Toward Reading Scale)	Reading	T=66, C=66
Taylor	1983	Traditional reading instruction (lecture, small group, large group, individualized) vs. instruction supplemented with structured CAI vs. instruction supplemented with unstructured CAI use; Pretest-posttest design (Nelson-Denny Reading Test)	Reading	T1=15, T2=14 C=12
Kochinski	1986	CAI remedial practice in reading vs. traditional remedial practice on reading achievement and self-concepts; pretest-posttest control group design (Gates-McGinitie Reading Test, Piers-Harris Children's Self-Concept Scale)	Reading	T=20, C=20
Ward	1986	CAI drill in reading skills vs. traditional practice with paper drill sheets; pretest-posttest control group design (Vocabulary test from basal reader, Math Attitude Scale)	Reading	T=26, C=25
McCormack	1985	CAI drill in letter-sound relationships vs. traditional drill; pretest-posttest design (Author-developed letter-sound test)	Reading	T=36, C=36
Hoffman	1984	CAI-supplemented reading instruction vs. traditional teacher-prepared supplements; pretest-posttest control group design (Gates-McGinitie Reading Test, Estes Attitude Scale)	Reading	T=51, C=45
Ortmann	1984	CAI-drill in reading skills vs. traditional drill; pretest-posttest control group design (CTBS)	Reading	T=118, C=232
Cooperman	1985	CAI-supplemented reading instruction vs. traditional classroom instruction; pretest-posttest design (California Achievement Test)	Reading	T=240, C=320
Coomes	1985	CAI-supplemented language and reading instruction vs. traditional instruction; pretest-posttest matched pairs design (CTBS)	Reading/ language	T=51, C=51
Summerville	1985	CAI-supplemented instruction in the Gas Laws vs. traditional classroom/lab instruction; pretest-posttest control group design (Items on the laws from the ACS/NSTA Examination)	Chemistry	T=51, C=41
* Melnick	1986	Logic games vs. math word problems vs. no additional instruction to increase problem-solving skills (Stanford math applications subtest and Stanford Achievement Test)	Math problem- solving	T1=52, T2=47 C=45

Grade Level	Treatment Length	Type CAI	Random Assign't	Computer Control?	Same/diff Teacher	Achieve-ment ES
4 Chapter 1	15 wks	Not described	N	N	Mixed	Overall=.18 Boys= .40 Girls=.10
College	51-78 hrs over qtr.	Drill Teacher-developed pgm.	N	N	Same	Overall=-.51 Struc.CAI=-.39 Unstruc.=-.64
Middle School (low achievers)	40 min/wk for 12 wks.	Drill: Alpine Skier, Steps to Comprehension, Calendar Skills	Y	N	Same	.00
4-6	60 min/wk for 4 wks	Drill Macmillan basal reader software)	Y	N	Different	Vocab.=1.48
K	30-10 min. sessions over 10 wks	Drill Hartley letter-sound relation-ship pkg.	Y	Y	Same	.85
5	10 min/day in 72 days	Drill: Misc. micro. reading, spelling pkgs.	N	N	Mixed	Overall=.03 Boys=.14 Girls=-.09
2-6	10 min/day for 1 yr	Drill (CCC)	N	N	Different	.62
2-4	10 min/day for 9 mons	Drill (PLATO)	N	N	Different	.09
4	30 min/wk for 1 yr	Drill: Misc micro.reading language pkgs.	N	Y	Different	.05
11-12	2-3 days	Simulations: Various pub.software	N	N	Same	.14
5	60 min./wk for 10 wks.	Logic games: The Factory & Code Quest	N	N	Different	vs. MP=.45 vs.Ctrl=-.05

Table 5 (continued)
Descriptions and Results of Dissertation
Studies in Instructional Computing

Study Author	Year	Description of Study Design and Focuses	Content Area	N
Mann	1986	LOGO programming vs. non-LOGO computer activities to improve problem-solving skills; matched pairs pretest-posttest control group design (Non-Verbal Battery of Cognitive Abilities Test)	Problem-solving	T=31, C=31
Fickel	1986	LOGO programming vs. computer control to improve students' problem-solving and cognitive skills; pretest-posttest control group design (Developing Cognitive Abilities Test & Nowicki-Strickland Locus of Control Scale for Children, Iowa Problem Solving Test, locally-designed LOGO test)	Problem-solving & locus of control	T=49, C=47
Olson	1985	CAI-supplemented instruction vs. LOGO-supplemented instruction vs. traditional textbook+manipulatives instruction; pretest-posttest design with repeated measures (Julian Elementary Test of Geometry Achievement, Monash Spatial Visualization Test, Crandall Intellectual Achievement Responsibility Questionnaire)	Geometric concepts	T1=14, T2=14 C=14
Shaw	1984	LOGO programmming vs. BASIC programming vs. control to improve problem-solving; non-equivalent control group design (New Jersey Test of Reasoning Skills)	Problem-solving	T(LOGO)=31, T(BASIC)=36,C=65
LeWinter	1985	LOGO programming-supplemented math instruction vs. traditional math instruction to improve attitudes and problem-solving; non-equivalent control group design (Dutton's Study of Attitude Toward Arithmetic, Crandall's Intellectual Achievement Responsibility Questionnaire, teacher-designed observations)	Problem-solving/locus of control, attitudes	T=174, C=98
Bamberger	1984	LOGO programming-supplemented math instruction vs. traditional math instruction to improve attitudes and problem-solving; post-test only control group design (Riedesel Inventory of Children's Attitudes Toward Math, investigator-designed PS measure)	Math problem-solving	T=15, C=15
Forte	1984	LOGO programming vs. CAI math drill vs. control to study effects on students diagnosed as "reflective" vs. "impulsive"; pre-test-posttest control group design (California Achievement Test, Matching Familiar Figures Test, measures of perceived self-confidence)	Math and cognitive skills	T1=13, T2=14 C=16

* Taken from Becker's charts (1987)

Grade Level	Treatment Length	Type CAI	Random Assign't	Computer Control?	Same/diff Teacher	Achieve-ment ES
8	10 wks	LOGO	Y	Y	Different	Overall=.50 Boys = .44 Girls = .54
6	30 min/wk for 32 wks	LOGO	Y	Y	Mixed	PS = .05 L of C = .18
6	6 wks	LOGO & various micro.software pkgs.	Y	Y	Different	LOGO vs.CAI=.05 LOGO vs.ctl=.02 CAI vs.ctl=.03 Girls = .09, .31, .18 Boys = .24, -.15, -.27
5	1 hr/day for 7 wks	LOGO & BASIC	N	N	Different	LOGO/BASIC=.29 LOGO/ctrl=.22 BASIC/ctrl=-.09
4-6	1 hr/wk for 12 wks	LOGO	N	N	Different	Locus=.167 (No data from PS observations)
4	30 min. 3 times/wk for 11 wks	LOGO	Y	N	Same	PS = .63
3	2 hrs/wk for 10 wks	LOGO and CAI drill (SRA Math)	Y	Y	Mixed	Overall math: LOGO & math=-.41 LOGO & ctrl=.77 Math & ctrl=1.09 Overall reading: LOGO & math=-.54 LOGO & ctrl=-.81 Math & ctrl=.39

Table 6
Descriptions and Results of Research on Attitudes Related to Computer Use in Instruction

Study Authors	Year	Description of Study Focuses
Meyer	1986	Attitudes toward graphics CAI vs. non-graphics CAI vs. regular instruction
Clarke	1985	Impact of Logo use on students' attitudes toward school subjects
Saracho	1982	Attitudes of Spanish-speaking migrant children toward CAI in groups who did/did not use CCC materials
D'Onofrio & Slama	1985	Preference for micro.vs.manual methods of learning accounting
Crawford	1984	Attitudes toward CAI in learning business math
Hedlund & Casolara	1986	Student attitudes toward computer use in psychology experiments
Wainwright	1985	Male/female attitudes toward CAI after chemical equations drill
Seymour	1986	Choice of learning medium for 2nd task after 1st task on computer or paper/pencil
Eisenberg	1986	Student preference of learning method after CAI drill use
Dalton & Hannafin	1986	Preference of instructional medium by three learning groups: video-only, CAI-only, interactive video
Goodwin et al.	1985	Students choice of learning tool after CAI use
Goodwin et al.	1986	Compared preferences of medium of students using/not using CAI
Zuk	1986	Preference for medium after reading stories on computer & book
Waldron	1985	Attitudes toward using computer-assisted graphics design tools
Menis	1984	"Scientific curiosity" and attitudes toward science of students using/not using CAI
Millman	1984	Math attitudes of students using CAI vs.paper/pencil drill
Turner	1986	Math attitudes after individual CAI use, paired CAI use, and regular classroom methods
Hawley et al.	1986	Attitudes toward math after CAI drill

Content Area	Total N (Approx.)	Grade Level	Results on Attitude Variables:			
			Computer Use in Instruc.	School & Subject	Self-esteem/ Confidence	Males vs. Females
Mathematics	T=29, C=33	1-5	Graphics=.89 Nongrap= -.40			
Math/problem solving	43	1, 3, 5	+			
Math/ reading	T=128, C=128	4-6	0.14			Males=.29 Females= -.01
Accounting	T=45,C=45	High school	0.27			
Business math	T=27,C=30	College	NSD			
Psychology	50	College	+			NSD
Chemistry	T=44,C=46	High school	- 0.51			Males= -.21 Females= -.81
Science	69, 70	5-6	+ (Most chose CAI)			NSD
Science	79	College	+			
Industrial arts	44, 44, 45	Jr.high	+ (CAI-only)			
Pre-reading	T=27, C=26	Pre-K	-			
Pre-reading	27, 26, 24	Pre-K	+			
Reading	55	3, 5	+			
Engineering	T=26,C=23	College		-		
Science	65	9		2.06		
Mathematics	T=19,C=20	LD/EMH		-0.26		
Mathematics	T=103, 105 C=105	3-4		Better w/ individual use		
Mathematics	T=39, C=40	3, 5		0.25		

Table 6 (continued)
Descriptions and Results of Research on Attitudes Related to Computer Use in Instruction

Study Authors	Year	Description of Study Focuses
Ward	1986	Attitudes toward math of students using CAI vs. paper drill
Ferrell	1986	Attitudes toward math after "total immersion" CAI use
Hamby	1986	Attitudes toward math after CAI in pharmacology math
Bamberger	1984	Math attitudes of students using Logo vs.traditional instruction
Lewinter	1985	Math attitudes of students using Logo vs.traditional instruction
Griswold	1984	Attitudes toward CAI of students using/not using CCC material
McDermott	1985	Student attitudes toward subject matter after CAI vs.reg.instruc.
Todd	1986	Attitudes toward subject matter of students using/not using CAI
Bryg	1984	Attitudes toward reading/school of students using/not using CAI
Hoffman	1984	Attitude toward reading of students using CAI vs. reg. instruc.
Moreland et al.	1987	Attitudes toward writing of students using/not using word processors
Cheever	1987	Attitudes toward writing of students using/not using word processors
Reimer	1985	Changes in students'self-concept of those using/not using Logo
Swaedner & Hannafin	1987	Self-confidence with computers: high/low achievers,males/females
Louie	1985	Effects of Logo use on students' self-acceptance
Kochinski	1986	Self-confidence in reading of students using CAI or reg.instruc.

Content Area	Total N (Approx.)	Grade Level	Results on Attitude Variables: Computer Use in Instruc.	School & Subject	Self-esteem/ Confidence	Males vs. Females
Mathematics	T=26, C=25	4-6		.81		
Mathematics	T=50, C=41	6		NSD		
Mathematics	T=32, C=32	College		0.16		
Math problem solving	T=15, C=15	3		0.32		
Problem solving	T=174, C=98	4-6		Overall=.15		Males=.37 Females=-.08
Math, reading	161	4-5		NSD	+	
Math Reading Lang.arts	T=1975,C=1778 T=1255,C=1343 T=1292,C=1370	3-6		0.42 0.37 0.29		
Mathematics Reading	123, 119	4		Math = .04 Reading=.47		
Reading	T=66, C=66	4		School=.21 Reading=.21		
Reading	T=51, C=45	5		Overall=.50		Males=.44 Females=.54
Writing	T=240,C=65	4-5		0.25		
Writing	T=25, C=25	4		+		
Math/ thinking	T=8, C=8	K			0.09	
Mathematics	32	6			+ (High achievers)	NSD
Problem solving	46	Secondary & elementary			-	
Reading	T=20, C=20	Middle school			-.25	

Table 6 (continued)
Descriptions and Results of Research on Attitudes Related to Computer Use in Instruction

Study Authors	Year	Description of Study Focuses
Anderson et al.	1980-81	Changes in self-esteem & other variables after simulation use
Collis	1985	Male vs. female confidence in using computers
Lloyd & Gressard	1984	Identification of variables correlating with high/low attitudes
Forte	1985	Correlated perceived self-confidence with various student characteristics

Content Area	Total N (Approx.)	Grade Level	Results on Attitude Variables:			
			Computer Use in Instruc.	School & Subject	Self-esteem/ Confidence	Males vs. Females
Science	369	9, 11			0.31	
Computer literacy	1800	12, 8				Females less confident
None	354	High school & college				NSD
Math, cognitive skills	43	3				High achievers had lower esteem

Computation of Effect Sizes

Standardized treatment effect sizes (ES) were computed by subtracting the mean gains (difference between pretest and posttest) of the control groups from those of the treatment groups and dividing by the pooled within group posttest standard deviations. Use of the pooled within group posttest standard deviations as divisors determines that these effect sizes are in final status form. Both Glass, McGaw, and Smith (1981) and Kulik and Kulik (1986) consider the final status scale to be more interpretable than those based on standard deviations of raw or residualized gains or covariance adjusted scores. Mean gains were used because in many studies that employed small sample sizes, there were substantial pretest differences between treatment and control groups, even though subjects had been assigned randomly to treatment conditions. In addition, a number of studies assigned treatments to intact groups so that initial non-random differences could have biased the posttest results. In a few studies, means and standard deviations were not available so effect sizes were computed from t or F statistics. The ES's obtained were corrected for small sample size bias, as recommended by Hedges and Olkin (1985).

Effect sizes were not corrected for unreliability or invalidity because the information necessary for such corrections was not generally available. Thus, they are probably conservative estimates of population values.

Analysis Requirements

Bangert-Drowns (1986) pointed out that each study in a meta-analysis should be represented only once in a statistical analysis because multiple effect sizes from any one study cannot be regarded as independent and should not be used in making statistical tests. In the present research, multiple effect sizes were averaged in the following ways: within content areas if there was more than one area (e.g., reading and mathematics) present, within sexes if results were reported by males and females, and within grades if results were reported by grade level. Thus, in most analyses, each study was represented only once. In some analyses, such as those comparing scores of males and females, each study was represented twice, but in these cases, each effect size in each study was based on a separate sample of subjects.

In a few instances, analyses were done to compare effect sizes where a study contributed data in all the categories analyzed. For example, in one analysis, effect sizes for reading comprehension, vocabulary, and word analysis were computed from data collected from single or overlapping student samples. The results of statistical tests used in these analyses must be interpreted with extreme caution because of this violation of the assumption of independence.

Analysis Steps and Procedures

The research questions explored in the present study were of two kinds. The first asked: "What is the overall effect size within a given content area or study feature condition?" The second was concerned with comparisons of ES's among levels of some study feature, e.g., "Are effect sizes the same for elementary, secondary, and college levels?"

The following steps were done in analyses to address the first kind of question. The numbers in parentheses following each description are the chapter and formula numbers given in Hedges and Olkin (1985) for performing the computations:

Step 1: A 95% confidence interval (CI) was computed for each study effect size (5-16). The CI shows the upper and lower limits within which the population effect size would fall in 95 of 100 replications of the study.

Step 2: The weighted average effect size (d+), which is an estimate of the population effect size, and its confidence interval were computed.

Step 3: The approximate CI's and ES's were plotted on one set of axes.

Step 4: The statistic Q (6-25) was computed to make a test of the homogeneity of the set of study effect sizes. If Q exceeded the 95% critical value of the chi-square distribution with k-1 degrees of freedom (where k is the number of studies in the set), the reviewers concluded that at least one study effect size differed from the others.

Step 5: If the set of studies was not homogeneous, the value of Q was recomputed, leaving out each study in turn. For these analyses, the reviewers developed and used a Basic program which indicated: whether or not the group of effects was homogeneous (Q), what Q would be if a given study were omitted from the analysis (Q_K), and the decrease in Q if the study were omitted (Q_R). It also computed the confidence intervals and effect sizes for the reduced set of studies.

Step 6: The set of Q_R values which were computed in Step 5 were used to identify studies that appeared to be outliers.

Step 7: The Q was recomputed for the reduced set of studies (after outliers were omitted). If it was significant, the process was repeated.

Step 8: Study features (other than the one of primary concern) of the group of outliers were examined to try to determine why their effect sizes were different from the larger set. The d+ for the whole set was compared with that of the reduced set.

To answer questions involving comparisons of effect sizes grouped according to levels of some study features, analyses using the following steps were done:

Step 1: Q_T and Q_W, the total and within group homogeneity statistics (7-23, 24, 25) and Q_B, the between group fit statistic (which is computed as Q_T-Q_W) were computed.

Step 2: The estimated population effect size for the entire set of studies (d++) was computed, along with the estimated effect sizes for each of the i groups. (d_i+).

Step 3: A chi-square table was entered with p-1 degrees of freedom for Q_B and k-p degrees of freedom for Q_W, where p is the number of groups and k is the number of studies in the entire set. If Q_W was significant at or less than .05, then a Q_{iW} for each group was computed and tested for homogeneity.

Step 4: Steps 5 through 8 above were followed to identify homogeneous subsets of effect sizes within each of the groups found not to be homogeneous.

Step 5: Q_T, Q_W, and Q_B were calculated over the homogeneous subsets within groups, and the appropriate statistical inferences were made. Also, d++ and d_i+ were recalculated, along with the confidence interval for each of them.

Step 6: Summary tables were prepared showing the Q statistics, their degrees of freedom, and their associated probability levels for both the entire set and reduced set.

Results for both the original set of studies and the reduced set are reported because there is disagreement among meta-analysis experts concerning the value of over-all homogeneity tests and outlier identification and because there is some subjectivity in determining which studies are outliers. Hunter, Schmidt, and Jackson (1983) do not use such tests because their power is so great that significant results may be seen as trivial. Their procedure is to try to eliminate variance across studies which is due to research artifacts such as sampling error, variation in criterion reliability and validity, variation in range restriction, and typographical errors in research reports. Hedges and Olkin (1985) advocate the use of tests of homogeneity and identification of outliers because they may identify effect sizes that "... differ from others in ways that are remediable" (e.g., they may represent mistakes in coding or calculation). Sometimes the diagnostic procedures point to a set of studies that differ in a collective way that suggests a new explanatory variable. Sometimes, of course, a study is an "outlier that cannot be explained by any obvious characteristic of the study" (Hedges and Olkin, 1985, p. 248).

REVIEW OF THE STUDY FINDINGS

In reviewing the 38 studies and reports and the 44 dissertations included in the meta-analysis for this study (Tables 4-6), one is struck immediately by the wide variation in study focuses, procedures, materials and findings. Seldom do any two studies focus on the same kind of topic using the same kind of target population, instructional materials, and achievement measures. If they do, their reports tend to differ considerably. Although over 80 studies with adequate data were able to be included in the achievement and attitude analyses, the absence of commonality among them makes it difficult to generalize across findings. The lack of standardization of data reported from study to study also severely hampers summarizing across studies. Therefore, the conclusions reached here must be viewed as tentative until more studies of similar types and with similar reporting styles are available to confirm or deny these trends.

Many of the findings of this study contrast sharply with those of past instructional computing meta-analyses. While Kulik's analyses found that dissertation results were significantly lower than those from other studies, the initial analyses in this review found that, while dissertation effects were slightly lower, they were not signficantly so. Therefore, dissertations were combined with the other studies for all subsequent tests of homogeneity. The topics covered by the various studies and the years they were reported are shown in Table 7 below. Some studies focused on more than one topic (e.g., both math and reading in the same study); therefore, the total number in some categories in this table is greater than the actual number of studies in the analysis.

Studies were categorized by grade level as elementary, middle/secondary, and college/adult. Grades 6 and 7 are a problem to categorize since they can be considered elementary or secondary, depending on the school's structure. A study was categorized as elementary if these were included with other elementary grades, and secondary if included with other secondary grades. If they were listed by themselves in a study, the study was categorized as middle/secondary.

Table 7 represents only the studies included in the meta-analysis. Many other studies were found which had insufficient data to include in the meta-analysis but are summarized here to give a more complete picture of the kinds of research being done in each area. In several cases, there is a discrepancy between the overall findings of studies included in the meta-analysis and those with anecdotal data. When this discrepancy occurs, the tendency of the reviewers is to give more weight to the group of studies presenting statistical data.

Table 7
Topics, Grade Levels, and Years of Study Reports
of Studies Included in Meta-analysis

	Math	TYPES OF SKILLS Read./ Lang.	Sci.	Cog. Skills	Other	GRADE LEVELS E	M/S	C/A	STUDY YEARS 80- 82	83- 84	85- 87
Dissertations	20	19	1	7	2	23	15	4	1	16	27
Other studies	16	14	4	9	1	21	7	6	5	9	24

As Table 7 indicates, most of the studies were either in reading or mathematics, and the majority of these were in basic skill areas. Also, if the sample for this review is any indication, research is on the rise in recent years, with almost three-quarters of the studies in the time reported during the period from 1985-87.

General Findings on Effectiveness

Available data indicate that computer applications have been effectively used in education, but more effectively in some areas than in others. The following sections provide tentative answers to some questions currently being asked about the general usefulness of computer applications in various grade levels, content and skill areas, and with various types of students.

Are Computer Applications More Effective at Certain Grade Levels?

Figures 2 and 3 show the results of an analysis comparing studies at elementary, secondary, and college/adult levels. Although effects at more than one level were often reported in one study, these levels can be included in the analysis because each effect was obtained from a separate sample of subjects. After an initial test of homogeneity indicated significant differences among effects within grade level groups, 21 studies with effects varying significantly from those of the general group were omitted for the second analysis (indicated in all the Figures with a special symbol). The effects and statistics resulting from these two analyses are shown in Table 8 below.

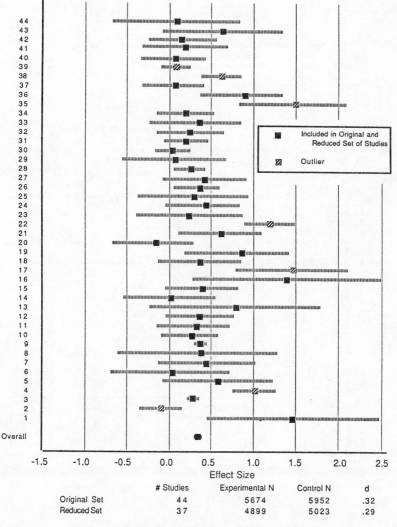

Figure 2. Effect sizes and confidence intervals found in elementary school studies

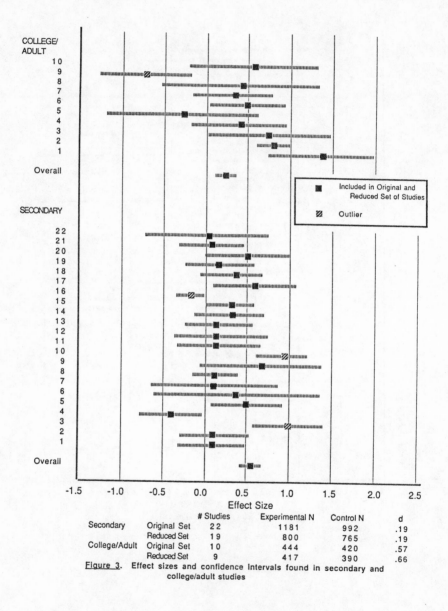

		# Studies	Experimental N	Control N	d
Secondary	Original Set	22	1181	992	.19
	Reduced Set	19	800	765	.19
College/Adult	Original Set	10	444	420	.57
	Reduced Set	9	417	390	.66

Figure 3. Effect sizes and confidence intervals found in secondary and college/adult studies

Table 8
Results of Tests Comparing
Elementary, Secondary, and College/Adult Effects

Source of Variation	Original Set				Reduced Set			
	Q	df	p	d+ (ES)	Q	df	p	d+ (ES)
Between groups	22.49	2	.05		29.61	2	.05	
Within groups	264.91	73	.05		77.72	52	.05	
Total	287.39	75	.05		107.33	54	.05	
Elementary	150.93	43	.05	.32	42.61	36	NS	.29
Secondary	73.91	21	.05	.19	19.86	18	NS	.19
College/Adult	40.07	9	.05	.57	15.25	8	NS	.66

d++ (Overall ES) = .31   d++ = .30

The results indicate that the effectiveness of computer applications varies significantly from level to level. This review found higher effects at college and adult levels (from .57 to .66), a direct contradiction with findings of past meta-analyses. The seven outlier studies with much larger effects than the others were compared for study features such as content/skill area, type of computer applications used, length of treatment, randomized sample, sample size, and same vs. different teacher. No similarities could be found which could explain the higher effects. A similar analysis performed on those outliers with lower effects had the same outcome.

Other characteristics in these studies might account for unusually high effects, but the variability of information in the study reports makes it difficult to ascertain what these charateristics might be. At this time, however, it appears that computer applications have a higher probability of meeting with greater success at college and adult levels than at elementary and secondary levels.

Are Computer Applications More Effective with Certain Types of Content?

Results for mathematics, science, reading/language, and for cognitive skills (such as general problem solving and critical thinking) are illustrated in Figures 4, 5, 6, and 7 respectively. Since these effects were often from the same study and the same sample, they were not independent observations and therefore could not be combined in one analysis. Thus, no between groups statistics are presented here. Table 9 below shows the results of the separate analyses.

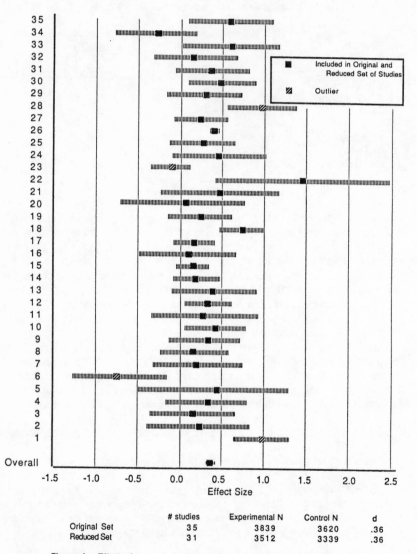

	# studies	Experimental N	Control N	d
Original Set	35	3839	3620	.36
Reduced Set	31	3512	3339	.36

Figure 4. Effect sizes and confidence intervals for all mathematics studies

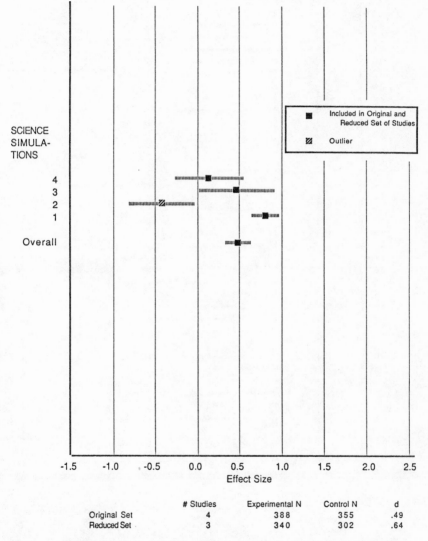

Figure 5. Effect sizes and confidence intervals in science simulation studies

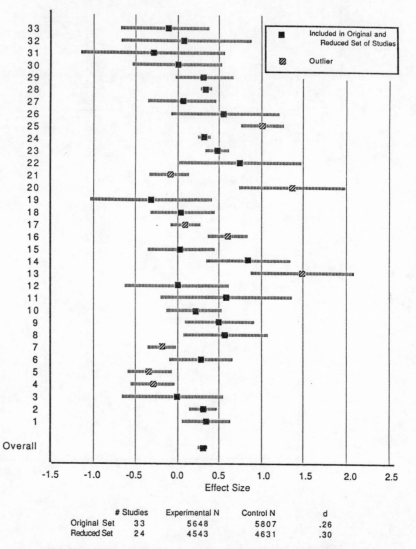

Figure 6.   Effect sizes and confidence intervals in all reading/language studies

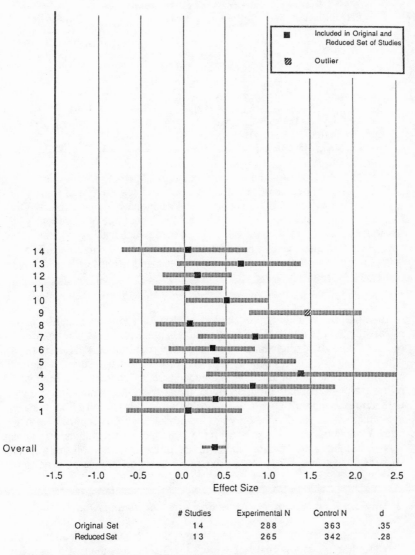

	# Studies	Experimental N	Control N	d
Original Set	14	288	363	.35
Reduced Set	13	265	342	.28

Figure 7.   Effect sizes and confidence intervals for problem solving/thinking studies

Table 9
Results of Tests Comparing Effects from Studies in
Mathematics, Science, Reading/Language, and Cognitive Skills

Source of Variation	Original Set				Reduced Set			
	Q	df	p	d+ (ES)	Q	df	p	d+ (ES)
Mathematics	94.58	34	.05	.36	37.67	30	NS	.37
Science	32.80	3	.05	.49	.64	2	NS	.64
Reading/language	183.43	32	.05	.26	32.35	23	NS	.30
Cognitive skills	23.82	13	.05	.35	12.78	12	NS	.28

Again, some surprising and unprecedented trends emerge from this review. Use of computer applications in math, reading, and cognitive skill areas all reflected similar effects, while science effects were nearly twice as great. Only four studies were included in the science analysis, but three of these four yielded moderately high positive effects. The outlier, which had a moderate negative effect, was also the only one of the studies which did *not* use a simulation in the study. In comparing computer drill to paper/pencil drill in chemical equations, Wainwright (1985) found that students preferred practice using the method with which they actually achieved significantly more: the non-computer method.

As in past meta-analyses, the mathematics studies yielded a slightly higher effect size than reading, but there was not as much gap between them in the present study. The mathematics and cognitive skill studies were fairly homogeneous, requiring only about 10% of the studies in each group to be omitted as outliers. Studies in the reading/language area, by contrast, had high variability. This was the only group in any of the analyses performed in this review with almost a quarter of the total studies differing substantially from the average effect size. It is also the only group with such a high proportion of negative effects (8 of 33 studies). As with the elementary level studies, an analysis was performed on the reading studies to determine any common study characteristics or features which could account for these differences, but no trends were apparent.

Are Computer Applications More Effective with Certain Kinds of Students?

A commonly-held belief in the literature about computer applications is that they are dramatically more effective with low achievers than with regular or high-achieving students. While this hypothesis has been substantiated in part by some past reviews, this study found no evidence of statistically significant differences between students on the basis of ability levels. Figure 8 shows the results of an analysis of effects for these groups, and Table 10 shows the statistics comparing the results of the groups. As Figure 8 indicates, the effects were fairly homogeneous in each group, and a total of only four studies were omitted for a second analysis. As with past groups, these outliers were compared to discover any common features which made them different from other studies, but none was found.

Table 10
Results of Tests Comparing Effects with
Low-Achievers vs. Regular Students

Source of Variation	Original Set				Reduced Set			
	Q	df	p	d+ (ES)	Q	df	p	d+ (ES)
Between groups	4.24	1	NS		4.60	1		NS
Within groups	99.55	42	.05		39.39	38	NS	
Total	103.80	43	.05		43.99	39	NS	
Low-achievers	23.92	14	.05	.45	9.57	13	NS	.36
Regular	75.63	28	.05	.32	29.82	25	NS	.22

(Overall ES) d++ = .34   d++ = .25

Another common hypothesis is that boys learn more with computer media, perhaps because it is socially more acceptable for them to use machines in other areas. The results of analyses for these groups are shown in Figure 9 and Table 11. The results of the second analysis, which omitted two outliers, indicate slightly higher effects for male students, but not significantly higher than those for females. However, the confidence interval for the effect size for females is not significantly different from zero at the .05 level. The fact that the difference between effect sizes for the two groups can be non-significant and yet only one is different from zero is statistically possible, especially with the small number of studies in the analysis. Yet it makes it difficult to draw any conclusions, even of a tentative nature, about the differences between these two groups. From the available data, one may conclude only that there is no firm evidence either than males do or do not achieve more than females with computer-based applications, and that the area needs further study.

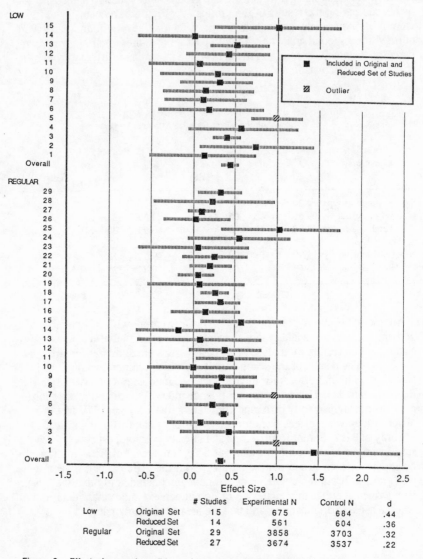

		# Studies	Experimental N	Control N	d
Low	Original Set	15	675	684	.44
	Reduced Set	14	561	604	.36
Regular	Original Set	29	3858	3703	.32
	Reduced Set	27	3674	3537	.22

Figure 8. Effect sizes and confidence intervals in studies of low vs. regular achievers

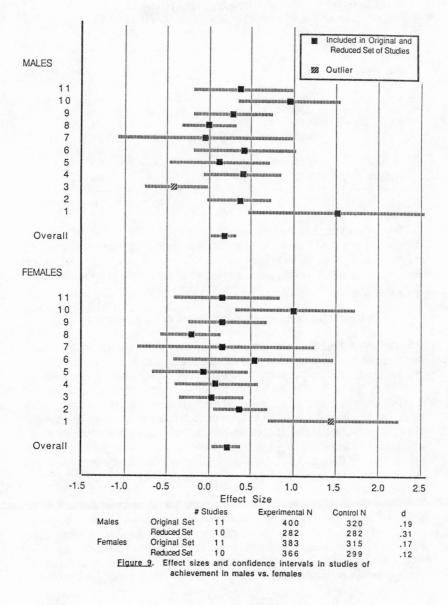

Figure 9. Effect sizes and confidence intervals in studies of achievement in males vs. females

		# Studies	Experimental N	Control N	d
Males	Original Set	1 1	4 0 0	3 2 0	.19
	Reduced Set	1 0	2 8 2	2 8 2	.31
Females	Original Set	1 1	3 8 3	3 1 5	.17
	Reduced Set	1 0	3 6 6	2 9 9	.12

Table 11
Results of Tests Comparing Achievement Effects with
Males vs. Females

Source of Variation	Original Set				Reduced Set			
	Q	df	p	d+ (ES)	Q	df	p	d+ (ES)
Between groups	.02	1	NS		2.67	1	NS	
Within groups	49.47	20	.05		26.22	18	NS	
Total	49.49	21	.05		28.89	19	NS	
Males	25.76	10	.05	.19	13.88	9	NS	.31
Females	23.71	10	.05	.18	12.38	9	NS	.12

(Overall ES) d++ = .18   d++ = .21

Other studies which had inadequate data to include in this meta-analysis concluded that males and females do not differ significantly in achievement involving computers. Webb (1984) found no significant differences between males and females in programming achievement, while Jones (1987) found no differences in mathematics achievement when CAI was used.

Do Student Attitudes Improve as a Result of Using Computers?

Since student attitudes have important implications for student learning, educators are as interested in effects in this area as they are in achievement. Several reasons account for this interest. Computers have long been found to be attractive to young people, and some researchers have tried to determine if students seem to prefer computer-based methods simply because a computer is involved. Because increased motivation to learn could translate into greater desire to stay in school, other studies have focused on computer influence on attitudes toward school and subject matter. Finally, research has grown out of the hypotheses of Papert (1980) and others that use of the computer in ways which emphasize students' control and creativity results in greater self-esteem and belief in their own abilities.

An analysis was performed of results reported on three groups of variables: self-confidence in learning or attitudes toward self, attitudes toward school or subject matter, and attitudes toward the computer as a medium of instruction. Few studies were found on the first and third of these variables, but those which were included were almost completely homogeneous. The second analysis needed to omit only one outlier. The results of the analysis are shown graphically in Figure 10 and numerically in Table 12. It should be noted that some of the effects on different variables are from the same studies; thus the results should be interpreted with caution.

Table 12
Results of Tests Comparing Effects of Computer Use on
Various Kinds of Attitudes

Source of Variation	Original Set				Reduced Set			
	Q	df	p	d+ (ES)	Q	df	p	d+ (ES)
Between groups	4.51	2	NS		.77	2	NS	
Within groups	23.77	16	NS		15.09	15	NS	
Total	28.28	18	NS		15.87	17	NS	
Toward self	2.90	2	NS	.25	2.90	2	NS	.25
School & subject	11.85	11	NS	.28	11.85	11	NS	.28
Computer medium	9.02	3	.05	.06	.36	2	NS	.19
(Overall ES) d++ = .23					d++ = .26			

The confidence interval for the group of two studies measuring attitudes toward the computer as a medium of instruction indicates that the effect size for this group is insignificant. This means that, on the basis of these few studies, students do not seem to have a preference for computers over other media. Greater effects were observed in studies focusing on effects of computer use on students' attitudes toward themselves and toward school learning.

Use of technological devices has been popularly perceived as a masculine domain, and some researchers feel that this could result in educational inequity. Therefore, effects on attitudes in males vs. females were also compared. Figure 11 and Table 13 show these results. Since there were only five studies which presented data separately for males and females, the analysis was not divided further into attitudes toward the three variables of interest. However, it should be noted that attitudes measured in these studies were usually toward school or subject matter. Findings for male vs. female attitudes are very similar to those for achievement. Males reflect slightly higher effects but not significantly higher. The effects were fairly similar within groups, and only one study had to be omitted for the second analysis.

Table 6 shows the results of all studies which were found in which student attitudes were measured in relation to some instructional use of the computer, including those which had only anecdotal data and, therefore, could not be included in a meta-analysis. In many cases, results of the statistical studies con-

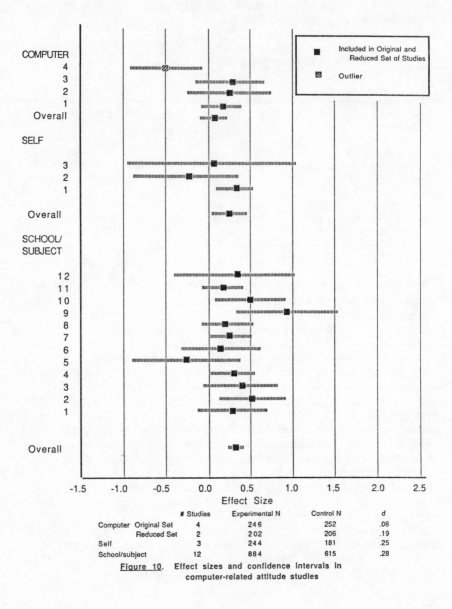

Figure 10.   Effect sizes and confidence intervals in
computer-related attitude studies

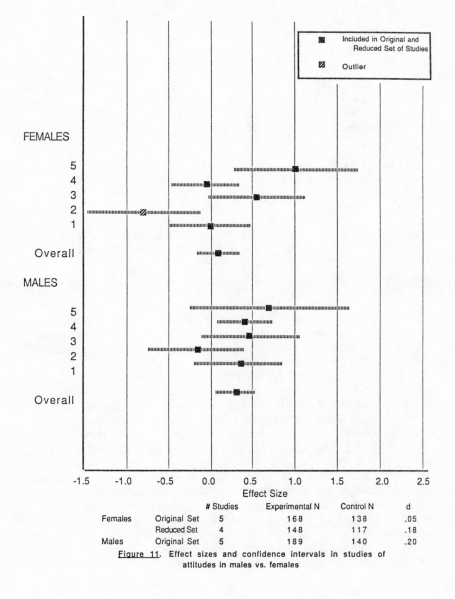

Figure 11. Effect sizes and confidence intervals in studies of
attitudes in males vs. females

flicted with those presenting anecdotal data. As was mentioned previously, the

Table 13

Results of Tests Comparing Effects of Computer Use
on Attitudes of Males vs. Females

Source of Variation	Original Set				Reduced Set			
	Q	df	p	d+ (ES)	Q	df	p	d+ (ES)
Between groups	2.17	1	NS		.44	1	NS	
Within groups	21.09	8	.05		12.83	7	N S	
Total	23.26	9	.05		13.27	8	N S	
Males	4.09	4	NS	.29	4.09	4	NS	.29
Females	17.01	4	.05	.05	8.74	3	NS	.18

(Overall ES) d++ = .18   d++ = .24

reviewers tended to give more weight to the group of studies which presented data to support their findings. Results of the anecdotal studies may be summarized as follows:

1. *Student preferences for computer methods* - Contrary to the findings of studies with statistical data, seven of the nine anecdotal studies which looked at student attitudes toward computer media reported that students preferred computer-based instruction. One surprising finding in three different studies was that students inexperienced in computer use or who did not get to use computers were more favorable toward them than students who had gotten a chance to use them, strongly suggesting a halo effect at work.

2. *Transfer of good attitudes toward computers to good attitudes toward subject matter and higher achievement* - Anecdotal studies yielded no additional evidence to support the belief that students' supposedly positive attitudes toward computers translate into more positive attitudes toward subject matter or to greater achievement. The exception to this general trend may be in use of word processing. Two different studies found that students liked word processing and, as a result, tended to want to write more. However, at the same time, the quality of writing did not seem to improve with word processsing use.

3. *Computer use and self-esteem* - Evidence from anecdotal studies did not give consistent support to the meta-analysis finding that use of computer applications helps students' self-concept. One study found positive results, one found positive results primarily with high achievers, and one (a Logo study) found negative impact.

4. *Differential effects with males and females* - While little evidence supports the belief that females' attitudes involving computer applications are less positive, one trend seems clear from anecdotal studies: females tend to have considerably less experience with computers and desire for such experience. Siann and Macleod (1986) note that this trend is true in both American and British studies and begins at early grade levels. They also note that females' disadvantage in this area "stems from a type of self-selection where females, even at primary levels, exclude themselves from technological areas," and that this self-selection has to do less with aptitude than with interest and perception of role. While this finding could have major impact on females' career choices, the current study found little to support the belief that negative attitudes of any group toward computers affects achievement.

Many more studies need to be done which collect data comparing computer and non-computer groups on these attitude variables. At this time, there appears to be insufficient rationale for selecting computer applications over another instructional medium in any content area on the basis of attitudes alone. The most promising of any area seems to be improving students' attitudes toward school and subject matter, especially in the area of using word processing with writing instruction.

Findings on Effectiveness in Specific Content Areas and Specific Student Groups

Information about the general effectiveness of computer applications is useful, but educators also need more specific data on which to base their decisions about how best to use computers in the future. For example, if personnel in a school district propose a program for using Logo to improve problem solving skills or for widespread use of microcomputer drill and practice to raise scores in basic math skills, administrators need to know what they can reasonably expect in terms of results from these programs. To answer these questions, data from the studies were analyzed in several different combinations.

It is worth mentioning again that the sketchy nature of the available data makes all these findings tentative at this time. With many of the studies, assumptions had to be made about the data in order to calculate effect sizes from them. For some studies, the reviewers had to contact authors directly to fill in missing information about procedures and findings. Often, the design of the study and/or the statistical analysis procedures could have been greatly simplified with no loss of utility or significance, and more frequently than one might expect with published studies and directed dissertation research, the authors failed to describe such basic information as the nature of the instruction for the control group or statistics such as standard deviations.

One particularly puzzling aspect which was found in several studies is that the conclusions reached by the experimenters seemed unrelated to the actual findings. For example, Saracho (1982) concluded that the use of CAI as a supplement to classroom instruction can significantly improve achievement even though the effect sizes calculated on her data were, in fact, small negative ones at three of the four grade levels tested. The remaining one was small positive (.13).

These characteristics, which were found in reports from both refereed and unrefereed sources alike, served to make results unclear and difficult to interpret. Despite these limiting features, a great deal of pertinent information was gleaned from the studies, and is reported here by content and skill areas of primary interest to educators.

How Effective Are Various Applications in Teaching Mathematics Skills?

Since there were so many studies in mathematics, a further analysis was done to determine if there were differences in effects among types of math skills and among the kinds of computer applications used in mathematics. Figure 12 and Table 14 summarize the findings comparing computer applications with lower level vs. higher level skills: computation vs. math concepts and problem solving. Effects between these two groups were found to be homogeneous, and no subsequent analysis needed to be done. These results indicate that computer applications are about equally effective with both groups of mathematics skills. However, these results must be viewed with caution since some studies measured both kinds of skills and therefore the data do not represent independent samples.

Table 14
Results of Tests Comparing Effects with
Two Kinds of Mathematics Skills

Source of Variation	Q	df	p	d+ (ES)
Between groups	.02	1	NS	
Within groups	11.60	11	NS	
Total	11.62	12	NS	
Computation	10.47	8	NS	.24
Concepts/ problems	1.13	3	NS	.26

(Overall ES) d++ = .25

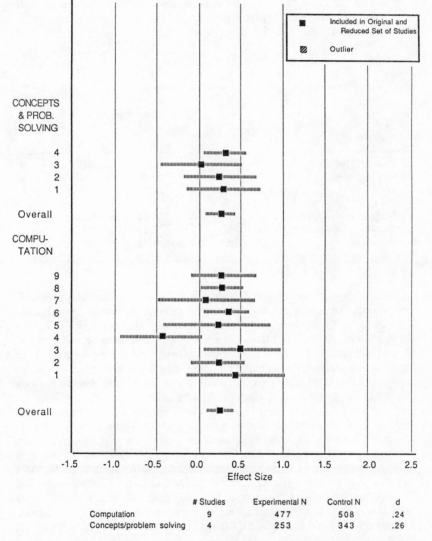

Although most studies were of drill applications, five studies were located which used tutorial materials and several others which used unstructured materials and tools of various kinds. The results of these comparisons are shown in Figure 13 and Table 15. With four outlying studies removed, there were no significant differences among the applications. The types of computer products were about equally effective.

Table 15
Results of Tests Comparing Effects from
Various Computer Applications in Mathematics Studies

Source of Variation	Original Set				Reduced Set			
	Q	df	p	d+ (ES)	Q	df	p	d+ (ES)
Between groups	.26	2	NS		2.48	2	NS	
Within groups	73.74	27	.05		22.08	23	NS	
Total	73.99	29	.05		24.56	25	NS	
Drill/practice	30.86	16	.05	.25	15.82	15	NS	.20
Tutorial	24.32	4	.05	.22	1.92	2	NS	.30
Other uses	18.55	7	.05	.20	4.35	6	NS	.38

(Overall ES) d++ = .24   d++ = .23

Several of the studies attempted to identify software characteristics which either enhanced or detracted from student achievement. In comparing drill software to mimeographed worksheets to enhance mathematics skills, Leigh, Horn, and Campbell (1984) found an effect size of .44, but observed that color graphics and personalized feedback actually tended to delay student progress. In a study which compared non-graphics and graphics software to paper worksheets for math practice, Carrier, Post, and Heck (1985) found an effect size of about half that much but noted that students were motivated by graphics and feedback features and were able to complete more practice problems on the computer than students who did problems on paper. A study by Fuson and Brinko (1985) had insufficient data to include in the meta-analysis, but they reported no discernible effect between use of flashcards vs. computer drill and found that the reasons students gave for justifying their preferences were strikingly similar for both the methods. Students in both groups said their medium was easier to use, more fun, and so on. Obviously, other factors such as student characteristics and instructional procedures were at work to affect performance and attitudes in these studies, but the researchers were unable to discover what they were.

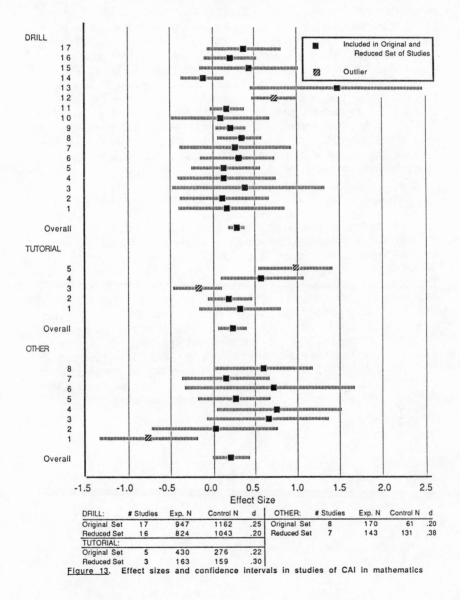

DRILL:	# Studies	Exp. N	Control N	d	OTHER:	# Studies	Exp. N	Control N	d
Original Set	17	947	1162	.25	Original Set	8	170	61	.20
Reduced Set	16	824	1043	.20	Reduced Set	7	143	131	.38
TUTORIAL:									
Original Set	5	430	276	.22					
Reduced Set	3	163	159	.30					

<u>Figure 13</u>. Effect sizes and confidence intervals in studies of CAI in mathematics

A study by Morehouse, Hoaglund, and Schmidt (1987) demonstrated vividly that unlimited access to the computer is no guarantee of instructional success. Although the computer-to-student ratio was very favorable, and software was selected and used extensively based on demonstrated student needs, the average effect size in mathematics was -.29. On the other hand, Henderson, Landesman, and Kachuk (1985) showed how effective computer applications can be when they are systematically designed and employed. They designed a video-tutorial which sequenced instruction based on learning hierarchies and designed presentations using methods based on proven-effective learning theories. Even the persons appearing in the videotapes were carefully "casted" to appeal to various elements of the student population. The result was a very successful program (ES=.98). This comparison may serve to demonstrate that the usefulness of all instructional media is highly dependent on careful design and implementation techniques.

How Effective Are Various Applications for Reading/Language Skills?

As with the mathematics area, the number of studies reported in reading and language made it possible to compare effects among types of skills and various kinds of computer applications in this area. The comparisons among skills were made even though the measures were frequently not independent ones. Therefore, the resulting tests of significance are not as reliable as the other comparisons made for this review, and the results are of limited usefulness. As Roblyer and King (1983) found in their meta-analysis of reading studies, computer applications seem most effective in the area of word analysis skills such as phonics, followed by higher level reading and language skills. Since there were only four studies in vocabulary and language areas, these effect sizes are very unreliable (Figure 14). However, the findings that word analysis skills profit significantly more than other reading skills from computer-based instruction is probably accurate, since it replicates previous findings (Figure 15).

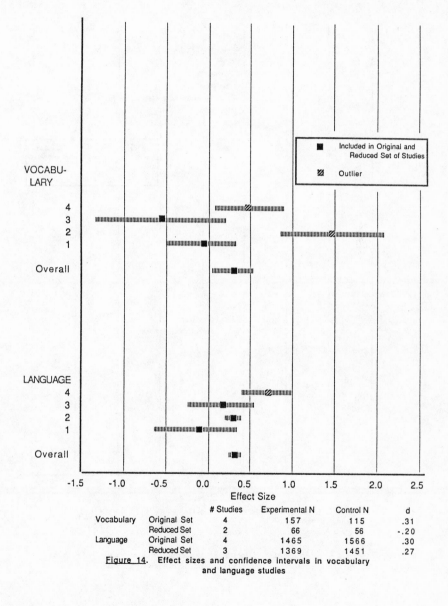

Figure 14. Effect sizes and confidence intervals in vocabulary and language studies

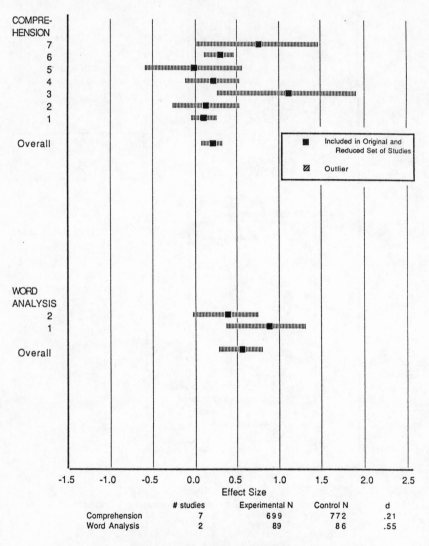

Figure 15. Effect sizes and confidence intervals in reading comprehension and word analysis studies

Table 16
Results of Tests Comparing Effects with
Various Reading/Language Skills

Source of Variation	Original Set				Reduced Set			
	Q	df	p	d+ (ES)	Q	df	p	d+ (ES)
Between groups	5.32	3	NS		10.80	3	NS	
Within groups	48.12	13	.05		18.14	10	NS	
Total	54.44	16	.05		28.94	13	NS	
Comprehension	10.37	6	NS	.21	10.37	6	NS	.21
Vocabulary	23.00	3	.05	.31	1.07	1	NS	-.20
Word Analysis	2.40	1	NS	.55	2.40	1	NS	.55
Language	12.36	3	.05	.30	4.29	2	NS	.27

(Overall ES) d++ = .28   d++ = .25

Many of the studies focused on both reading and mathematics skills, frequently using one group to control for the other to decrease the possibility of Hawthorne effects from computer use in the experimental group. In these studies, reading effects are consistently lower than those for mathematics. In studies by Williams (1985) and Todd (1986), which both used the same software, reading effects were negative (-.31 and -.35), while mathematics results were much higher (.17 and .74). Since software from the same source was often used for both content areas in other studies (e.g., Computer Curriculum Corporation software), it seems unlikely that software and usage differences account for this trend. On the basis of these rather consistent findings, it appears that computer applications work better for mathematics than for reading instruction.

Like the overall area of reading/language, the studies in the analysis for types of CAI in reading reflected great variability (Figure 16). Nearly 40% of the studies using drill and practice had to be omitted to achieve homogeneity. An analysis of outliers found that studies with higher effects usually had non-computer control groups. From these rather limited results, tutorial uses seem more effective than other computer applications, although the difference among types was not significant.

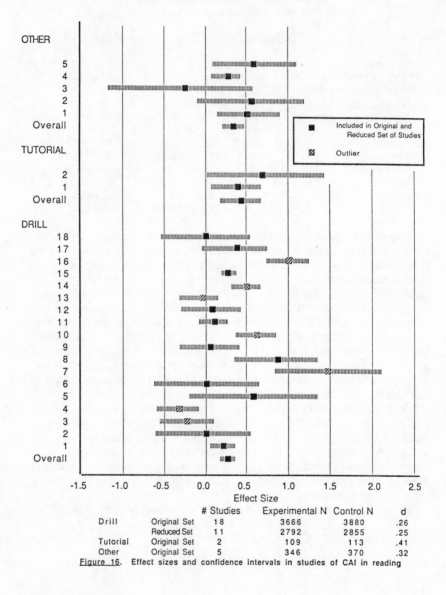

Figure 16. Effect sizes and confidence intervals in studies of CAI in reading

Table 17
Results of Tests Comparing Effects from
Various Computer Applications in Reading/Language Studies

Source of Variation	Original Set				Reduced Set			
	Q	df	p	d+ (ES)	Q	df	p	d+ (ES)
Between groups	1.72	2	NS		2.05	2	NS	
Within groups	134.01	22	.05		22.15	14	NS	
Total	135.82	24	.05		24.20	16	NS	
Drill/practice	128.03	17	.05	.26	16.08	10	NS	.25
Tutorial	.89	1	NS	.41				
Other uses	5.18	4	NS	.32				

(Overall ES) d++ =.27   d++ =.26

How Effective Are Computer Applications in Science?

As was mentioned in the section on general findings, results in the science area were especially promising even though only four studies were located to include in the meta-analysis. (See Figure 5 and Table 18.) It is worth noting again that the only study which did not have a positive effect was one in which students used drill and practice in balancing chemical equations (Wainwright, 1985). Moore, Smith, and Avner (1980) found that students achieved significantly more with computer methods with simulations only when they used them to interpret results and make decisions about the simulated experiments. When students were required only to follow directions and calculate results in this study, no differences between experimental and control groups were found. Moore et al. believe this indicates that computer applications are significantly more effective with higher level skill lab work, rather than structured practice activities. The other studies by Summerville (1985) and Fortner, Schar, and Mayer (1986) confirmed this trend, but further studies need to be done to replicate this finding.

Table 18
Results of Tests Comparing Effects with
Science Studies

Source of Variation	Original Set				Reduced Set			
	Q	df	p	d+ (ES)	Q	df	p	d+ (ES)
Science	32.80	3	.05	.49	8.36	2	NS	.64

How Effective Are Computer Applications in Teaching English and Reading to ESL Students?

Just as the small number of studies in science calls into question the overall high effect size from these studies, the fairly low effects found over the three studies in the ESL area must also be viewed with caution. First, the study effects were quite heterogeneous (Figure 17), with one obtaining positive and two negative effect sizes. Another interesting finding is the comparison between two of the studies (Ojeda, 1984 and Noda, 1983) who both used the same kind of materials and the same measure of achievement (California Achievement Test). Ojeda's study with Spanish-speaking students yielded an effect size of -.19 and Noda's with Arabic/Chaldean students found one of .60. Their research designs and sample sizes were also different, and these population and study implementation features may account for the different results.

Table 19
Results of Tests Comparing Effects with
ESL Studies

Source of Variation	Original Set				Reduced Set			
	Q	df	p	d+ (ES)	Q	df	p	d+ (ES)
ESL	8.05	2	.05	-.06	.19	1	NS	-.15

Another study included in the meta-analysis under the reading area reported data for Hispanic vs. Anglo students in CAI and control groups, but they were not reported in such a way that just the data for Hispanic students could be included in the ESL analysis. In this case, Ortmann (1984) found that Hispanic

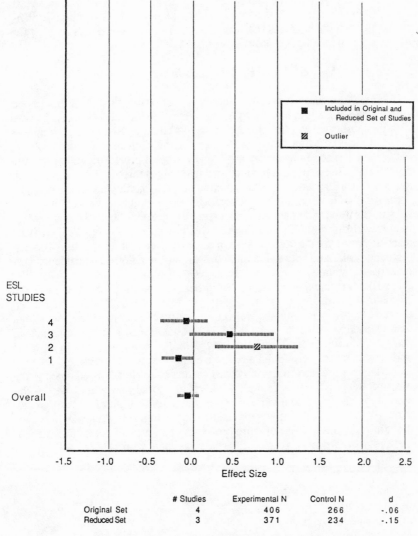

Figure 17. Effect sizes and confidence intervals in ESL studies

students achieved better gains than Anglos in both CAI and non-CAI groups, but that there were no differences between gains of Hispanics in CAI and non-CAI groups. Although standard deviations were not present, the mean scores in these groups indicate that the effect size would have been a negative one, if it had been calculated. The overall picture in studies of CAI with Spanish-speaking students suggests that CAI does not seem to have advantages for them over other methods in learning English skills.

How Effective Is Word Processing in Improving Writing Skills?

One ebullient author compared the realization that the business tool called word processing could be used to teach composition to the discovery that the volatile substance used for Chinese fireworks could also be used as gunpowder. On the other hand, Harris (1985) termed the claims about word processing "extravagant and unsubstantiated." Indeed, word processing seems to have had an explosive impact on instructional methods in this area, as well research and debate on its usefulness. Its attraction lies in its ability to take the physical "drudgery" of handwriting out of composition. In light of this fact, it is perhaps not as important that word processing has greater effects on achievement than traditional methods, but merely that they be equivalent. Still, writing teachers have hypothesized that use of these tools can improve quality of writing, length of compositions, number and kind of revisions, and students' attitude toward writing.

Nearly all of the studies which could be included in the meta-analysis focused on the variable of writing quality. As Figure 18 and Table 20 indicate, the effects from these studies were completely homogeneous and yielded an overall positive effect size, with a 95% probability of being different from zero. Even Morehouse et al. (1987), who found negative effects in all other math and reading areas, found a positive effect with word processing. Its positive effects on students' attitude toward writing have already been noted in the previous section. Harris (1985), whose study could not be included in the meta-analysis, found that one reason for this improved attitude was that students liked the "clean copy" produced by the computer. This was true even though she found that use of word processing had little effect on making students revise more or take more risks and experiment with writing.

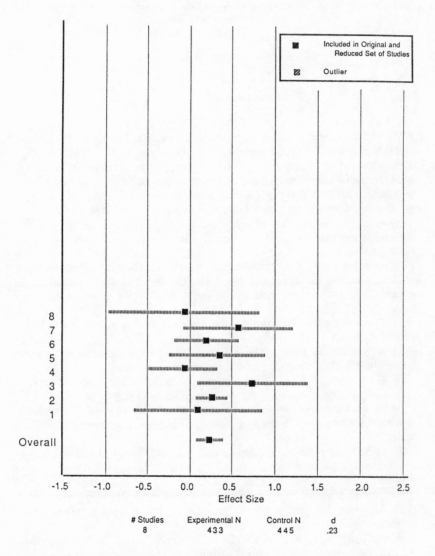

# Studies	Experimental N	Control N	d
8	433	445	.23

<u>Figure 18</u>. Effect sizes and confidence intervals in word processing studies

Table 20
Results of Tests Comparing Effects with
Word Processing Uses

Source of Variation	Q	Original Set		d+ (ES)
		df	p	
Word processing	6.85	7	NS	.23

The general trend in other studies which were not included in the meta-analysis was that word processing use had little impact on the number of revisions or on increasing the quality of revision strategies, although it did tend to increase the number of words per composition that students produced. Some researchers noted that if the word processor included a spelling checker, the number of errors in compositions could be significantly reduced.

Hawisher's (1986) review of research on word processing describes clearly the implementation differences among studies which could seriously affect findings. Her comments also accurately describe the sample of studies in this review, and serve to illustrate the problem in summarizing across research studies, not only for word processing uses but for computer applications in general. Hawisher notes some of the variables affecting achievement other than the word processing use itself:

1. *Types of tools* - Word processors vary considerably in features and ease of use.

2. *Composing vs. transcribing* - Typing in already-written compositions is a very different task from composing at the word processor.

3. *Writing tasks* - The number of writing samples gathered and the type of writing students were asked to do varied from study to study.

4. *Measures of writing achievement* - Studies differed greatly in both the writing achievement variables they considered and the ways they assessed each variable.

The amount of prior experience students had with the word processing system was also mentioned by other authors as a factor influencing the outcome of a study. Clearly, summaries across studies which are similar in some or all of these variables would be more helpful than mere estimates of general usefulness in advising the practitioner on how to use word processing to best advantage.

Work is also being done on a variety of other interesting topics which could eventually prove helpful to writing instructors. The following are a sampling of research directions which seem to have promise for helping educators real-

ize the potential of word processing for writing instruction. Daiute and Kruidenier (1985) have studied the effects of a word processor which incorporates
a question-prompt feature to help students read and analyze their own writing
and consequently improve their revision processes. Rubin and Bruce (1984)
describe problems inherent in getting children to express their thoughts in writing and the features which can be built into a word processor to address each
of these problems. Rosegrant (1986) has studied the role of speech synthe-
sized feedback to young children as a method of enhancing text revision. Finally, Pea and Kurland (1984) describe a process of using word processors in
a way which connects the activities of thinking with those of writing.

How Effective Are Logo and CAI Applications to Teach Problem-solving?

Perhaps no single application of computers in education has provoked more
widespread interest among educators or more controversy about its effects on
students than Logo, a programming language designed by Seymour Papert in
the late 1970's. As Becker (1987) found in a 1985 survey of instructional
computer uses, more than 40,000 educators across the country--about 9% of
all computer-using teachers--are using it, in addition to uncounted others outside the U.S. Books have been written on the subject, conferences have been
held on its various uses, and a seemingly endless flow of dissertations have
been generated which focus on effects hypothesized for it. However, as has
been widely observed (Pea, 1987; Walker, 1987), research outside the doctoral thesis requirement has not kept pace with the interest in Logo.

Probably the main reason for both the widespread use of Logo and the lack
of research data thereon arises from the same source: the writings of its originator. In his book *Mindstorms* (1980), Papert extols the potential benefits of
Logo, emphasizing especially the skills and attitudes related to problem solving
which he feels students acquire from its use and which he hypothesizes will
transfer to their other school work and life experiences. The attractiveness of
his claims and the enthusiasm and certainty with which he makes them are
most likely responsible for the popularity of Logo among practitioners. And,
of course, educators, after years of criticism of their approaches and results,
are eager to hear of a means of revitalizing instructional methods and creating
more interest in learning on the part of students. In essence, Papert's vision of
Logo in schools seems to hold this promise.

But at the same time, in language just as decisive and sure, Papert labels as
ineffective the practice of using experimental methods to investigate the effects
of Logo applications in classrooms. His reasons may be summarized in three
points. He feels that:

1. Other kinds of information gathering methods, namely, dialogs with
teachers and anecdotal evidence, will make research studies unnecessary.

2. Traditional behavioral research methods are too narrow in their view of Logo's instructional complexities and outcomes since they are "based on a concept of changing a single factor in a complex situation while keeping everything else the same" (Papert, 1987).

3. The Logo experience for each child is too unique to study and make statements about in common terms.

Many educators who have been involved with educational research for many years are quick to point out flaws in this line of reasoning and call for an increase in research on Logo effects. In response to Papert's view that systematic research methods are unnecessary to support his claims, Walker (1987) points out that human judgement is prone to bias and error, and that "to be taken seriously, such claims must be backed up by serious work, not just the impressions of the committed." Pea (1987) also observes that Papert's view of all research methods as activities which try to isolate and study only one small factor of a given situation is misinformed, since "one can also do multivariate instructional experiments in which many cultural features change without 'keeping everything but one factor constant' " (p. 6), thus allowing an experimenter to investigate complex phenomena in a realistic way.

Finally, as Walker (1987) notes, although many aspects of each student's classroom experience are unique, they hold many in common with other students in other classrooms. As Walker states, "It is an important task of inquiry to discover the order found in classrooms where Logo plays a prominent role and how that order compares to other classrooms" (p. 10). Clearly, systematic research into the effects of Logo in various settings and with various methods of implementation is an essential activity if we are to make any progress toward identifying specific benefits and establishing guidelines for maximizing these benefits.

From Papert's descriptions and subsequent ones by educators who have applied his theories in practical settings, hypotheses about Logo's effects can be derived. First, Logo, especially when implemented in the discovery-learning environment recommended by Papert, is hypothesized to make students acquire certain cognitive capabilities which can be brought to bear on solving problems in many kinds of content areas, not just obvious ones as mathematics or other programming. Second, the Logo environment is posited to bring about a more positive mindset in students, increasing their self-esteem and making them more likely to want to solve problems and increasing their motivation to learn.

We have already discussed the results of a few studies which could be located on the effects of Logo on students' self-esteem. Using a variety of measures of self-concept, some studies found positive results, some negative, and some no effect at all. The only study on which an effect size could be calculated for self-concept was Reimer's (1985) study, and it yielded a small effect size (.07) which was not significantly greater than zero. Thus, no conclusions can be drawn about the impact of Logo on students' image of themselves on the basis of evidence available at this time.

As for the effects on problem-solving and general thinking skills, they are shown in Figure 19 and Table 21 in comparison with effects from so-called "problem-solving CAI." The latter are unstructured materials such as "Rocky's Boots" and "Snooper Troops" which usually call for a discovery-learning approach.

Table 21
Results of Tests Comparing Effects on Cognitive Skills
Studies Using Logo and Problem-solving CAI

Source of Variation	Original Set				Reduced Set			
	Q	df	p	d+ (ES)	Q	df	p	d+ (ES)
Between groups	1.53	1	NS		5.78	1	.05	
Within groups	28.13	13	.05		12.41	12	NS	
Total	29.66	14	.05		18.19	13	NS	
Logo use	12.07	10	NS	.39	12.06	10	NS	.39
CAI	16.06	3	.05	.20	.34	2	NS	-.01

(Overall ES) d++ = .32   d++ = .26

These results, as measured by a variety of tests from experimenter designed rule-using and problem-solving tasks to the New Jersey Test of Reasoning Skills, indicate a fairly substantial and homogeneous effect for Logo in enhancing problem-solving skills. In most of these studies, Logo was compared with no additional instruction, with additional mathematics instruction, or with another programming language like Basic. However, a study by Dalton (1986) compared Logo with a curriculum specifically designed to improve problem-solving skills. While data were insufficient to include in the meta-analysis, Dalton reported that the problem-solving program group achieved significantly more than the Logo or control groups at every level of student ability.

Only four studies could be located for CAI applications to problem-solving and thinking skills, and the trend of effects in these studies was not as high. Only one study had a high effect size, and two of the others had negative ones. On the basis of these findings, Logo shows promise as a method of enhancing cognitive skills of various kinds, and looks especially good in comparison with unstructured, discovery-learning CAI applications. However, more studies need to be done comparing Logo with non-computer problem-solving pro-

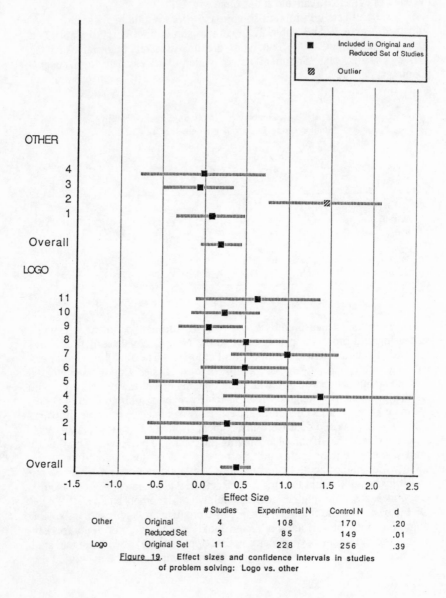

		# Studies	Experimental N	Control N	d
Other	Original	4	108	170	.20
	Reduced Set	3	85	149	.01
Logo	Original Set	11	228	256	.39

Figure 19.   Effect sizes and confidence intervals in studies
of problem solving: Logo vs. other

grams of instruction, as Dalton did.

Can Computer Applications Increase Student Creativity?

Students' creative abilities are regarded by some as innate aptitudes and by others as skills which can be taught. Materials of various kinds have been developed through the years to try the latter approach, with varying (and often undocumented) success. In addition to claims that Logo can enhance problem-solving skills and self-concept, Logo proponents have also hypothesized capabilities for use of the programming language in this area.

Only three studies--all Logo-based--could be located to include in the meta-analysis on this area. Reimer (1985) and Clements and Gullo (1984) used the Torrance Tests of Creativity, and Horton and Ryba (1986) measured creativity with a locally-developed test involving creation of a line drawing. Perhaps it will come as a surprise to the anti-Logo educators, but the results across this limited sample are homogeneous and consistently high as Table 22 indicates, with an overall effect higher than any other found in this review. Unfortunately, it is not possible to conclude that Logo is more effective than another non-computer treatment, since experimental Logo groups were often compared with no-instruction control groups. Conclusions are further limited by the fact that sample size in each of the three studies is eight or nine per group. Thus, the resulting confidence interval shown in Figure 20 indicates the effect, while significantly different from zero, could be anywhere from .15 to 1.30.

Table 22
Results of Tests Comparing Effects on
Student Creativity

Source of Variation	Q	Original Set		d+ (ES)
		df	p	
Creativity	.11	2	NS	.73

These results, while promising, are in need of further study, preferably with larger sample sizes and control groups which use other forms of instructional treatment. Researchers may find that it is the small class size, rather than the use of specific tools, which makes possible the high effect sizes.

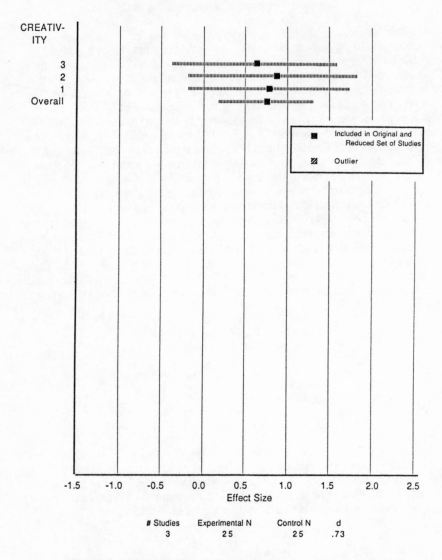

Figure 20. Effect sizes and confidence intervals in studies on creativity

Procedures and Findings of Major Studies

Several of the studies in this review merit a more in-depth discussion of their research questions, methods, and findings. These are the major, long-term research activities which should be of interest to many educators and decision-makers in the field, not only for their results, but also for the models which their designs and procedures provide to others wishing to do research on similar questions or content areas.

The ETS/LAUSD Study:
The Computer Curriculum Corporation (CCC) System and
Compensatory Education

This major three-year study represents one of the largest, most comprehensive computer-based studies ever undertaken. Although it was discussed in the first section of this review under previous meta-analyses, it was not included in the current analysis of data for several reasons. First, it was initiated in 1976 and its directors reported results for the first time in 1979. Second, since it was a study from the time period prior to 1980, its data were also included in many previous meta-analyses. Finally, it represents an older, non-microcomputer technology which was not emphasized in this review. However, it is a significant study, and its methods and findings should be of use to many decision-makers contemplating the purchase of a CCC system. The CCC program has been studied many times, but never so thoroughly and systematically as by ETS for the Los Angeles Unified School District. The findings of this study are probably the most reliable one could wish for on this particular kind of product.

The CCC curricula used in this study were drill and practice activities in mathematics (Grades 1-6), reading (Grades 3-6), and language arts (Grades 3-6). The ITBS, CTBS, and Curriculum-Specific Tests were used as pretests and posttests to measure achievement. The study took place in six schools, four of which received CAI and two of which acted as controls. As Ragosta (1980) reported, alternate groups of students in the four CAI schools either received CAI or acted as cohort controls without CAI. This arrangement resulted in three kinds of controls:

1. *Within CAI controls* - The mathematics and reading students served as controls for each other.

2. *Cohort controls* - Alternate cohorts of students in CAI schools received no CAI. These acted as controls for other students in the same school who were receiving CAI.

3. *Comparison school cohorts* - Students in the non-CAI schools acted as

controls for those receiving CAI.

To use CCC, schools had to implement a "pull-out program," requiring students to use the system for drill 10 minutes each per school day. Over 2000 students were involved in the study over the three-year period. The schools had to be renovated to house the CAI labs, teachers had to be trained, classroom procedures modified, and the research design had to be maintained over an extensive period. As Ragosta noted, the study was "a true social experiment." One of the most useful aspects of the study as described in the report was the detailing of all the planning, preparation, and logistics of upkeep required for this major intervention, and the reactions of students and teachers to it all. Even if no effectiveness data had been collected, this information makes fascinating reading for school districts considering such an undertaking.

As Glass noted in his chapter in Ragosta's report, the corrected effect sizes estimated from the CAI vs. cohort control design were about .45 for math computation skills, around .10 for math concepts and applications, and about .15 for both reading and language. Reading effects were highly variable across the studies, making summarizing risky, and these test scores were apparently affected by a mismatch between the language curriculum and the language subtests. As a result of these factors, only the math computation area yielded an effect size significantly different from zero. Glass could find no trends in CAI usage (grade level, duration of instruction, etc.) which correlated with higher or lower effect sizes. In light of these findings, Glass's conclusion is that other less-expensive methods should probably be examined as alternatives for CAI.

The ETS Writing-to-Read Study

If the ETS/LAUSD study is one of the most significant studies in the pre-microcomputer era, the ETS research on IBM's Writing-to-Read system is a hallmark of research for the current era in educational technology. This study involved 10,000 children at the kindergarten and first grade levels in 28 sites over a two year period. This effort, too, required extensive changes to the schools, curricula, and school procedures. Often described as a supplemental reading program, WTR requires much more modification of the teacher's instructional plan than does the CCC system. The computer is used primarily for phonics drill and management of student records in WTR, and thus is only a small component in a multi-method/media program.

The research design is described by Murphy and Appel (1984) as a pretest-posttest design in which standardized measures of reading and language selected by the districts involved were used as pretests and posttests. A specially-designed writing analysis method was also used as a posttest. Data were collected primarily from the kindergarten level, and were gathered by racial, gender, and SES groups.

The following are some of the general findings of this important study:

1. *Effects by school site* - Although the average effect across reading and writing was about .28, there was a wide range of effects (-.21 to 1.02) across sites. Also, Murphy and Appel report that effects were positive in 29 of 33 schools, and this means that WTR compared unfavorably with other programs in four schools. Clearly, other factors (e.g., student characteristics, teacher methods) besides the curriculum were at work to cause this variability.

2. *Effects by skill* - Writing tended to have greater effects than reading (.38 vs. .18). Murphy and Appel report that the impact on writing at early ages was great on both development of skill and children's perceptions of their writing abilities. The teachers and administrators at WTR sites also felt very positive about effects on writing.

3. *Effects by group* - The researchers note the following concerning subgroups of students in the study: "When the impact of WTR was examined for subgroups of children, it was found that the impact was generally significant for the subgroups where it was significant for the entire group. However, the size of the impact varied. For minority children and low SES children, the impact was less. In the case of below average children, teachers cautioned in their responses to our survey that WTR did not appear to be as effective for below average children as for above average children. There is evidence in the ETS data to support this assertion" (p. 6.5).

The latter observation may be a most important one. This study may illustrate what instructional designers have been saying for years: it is nearly impossible to design an extensive curricular intervention which suits all students equally well. While Murphy and Appel report that "there is good evidence that Writing to Read had a powerful impact on the learning of the children" (p. 6.1), the results may indicate that this program works best with white, on-or-above grade-level students.

Three Studies of Technology-Intensive Programs

Having enough computers to serve all the needs of one's students is a rare situation in most American schools. Many books have been written in recent years on how to maximize scarce resources and still do instructionally meaningful activities with microcomputers. Improving the student-to-computer ratio is an on-going mission for the majority of computer-using teachers. The hypothesis is implicit in these efforts that increased access to microcomputers will mean greater impact on student achievement. The goal, however distant it may be for many schools, seems to be one computer for each student in a classroom or laboratory at a given time.

Several studies have focused on this issue of what constitutes adequate access, and what one might expect with various ways of implementing micro-computers in schools. Each of the three reported here represents an unusually well-funded project in which a state agency or school sponsored an evaluation to determine future directions for the microcomputer program.

Project IMPAC

McDermott (1985) produced a particularly well-documented account of Project IMPAC (Instructional Microcomputer Project for Arkansas Classrooms), a major research study of four different, but equally intensive, delivery systems for integrating microcomputers into classroom instruction. Each of these systems was set up to allow one student to each computer for a certain length of time each day or week.

1. C-CAI - Four microcomputers in a single classroom were used to present three types of software: comprehensive (apparently tutorial), single-concept, and game-based. Students used computers from 3-10 days in a ten-day cycle for about 12-20 minutes per day of use.

2. A-CAI - Eight microcomputers in a network with a hard disk were placed in self-contained or semi-departmentalized classrooms in which teachers worked with 2-3 mathematics groups. Again, students were placed on a ten-day cycle of computer use, and used computers varying numbers of days in that cycle for 12-20 minutes per day. Two comprehensive mathematics packages were used, one tutorial and one apparently drill.

3. A-CMI-CAI - Twenty-four microcomputers were placed in a classroom, thus making it into a lab. Classes of students were brought to the lab, using the computers for 15-25 minutes per day for 8 days of 10. The same software was used as in the A-CAI treatment.

4. C-AIM - Eight computers were networked and connected to a hard disk and a printer. A locally-developed software package called C-AIM was used to monitor student progress, and some CAI was used to supplement the traditional mathematics program. The same time schedule as described in A-CAI above was used.

In all these treatments, software was carefully selected and matched to Arkansas Basic Skills and to the SRA Achievement Test, the measure used in the study. Like the ETS/LAUSD report, this document is a gold-mine of information on how to set up a system-wide program of this kind and evaluate its impact on students and schools. It also addresses the concern of cost-effectiveness, an often-neglected topic in studies of this kind.

Average effect sizes in mathematics varied widely (.02 to .62), with the most favorable results coming from the C-AIM treatment of traditional instruction supplemented by CAI. The report indicated that the State of Arkansas was moving forward with the IMPAC Project "with caution." McDermott did not recommend a state-wide implementation of the project at that time with the hardware and software that was currently available. Instead, he indicated that some additional programs would be added to the project and planning would begin for computer uses in Grades 9-12. Perhaps most important, McDermott noted that, "As educators, we must use common sense with respect to innovations. The human element must not be overlooked--the teacher cannot be replaced. Technology must be a servant to the teacher, and the wise use of technology by the teacher provides a way for more direct involvement between teacher and pupil--more one-on-one contact--not less" (p. 132).

Computer Immersion Project

Ferrell (1986) referred to her study as a "computer immersion project," since it was an attempt at providing all of the computer resources and time on the computer which a classroom could ask for. The purpose was to determine whether supplying large amounts of instruction via CAI when adequate resources were present would result in greater achievement. Ferrell also wanted to see if attitudes, attendance, and discipline would be affected by the predominantly computer-based method.

In this sixth grade study, the computer-to-student ratio was 1:1, and students received mathematics instruction almost exclusively with microcomputers for a full year. The control group received traditional teacher-directed, group-centered instruction. Although the experimental group did significantly better than the control group (ES = .48), Ferrell found that the majority of the effect was in raising computation scores, a result which duplicates Glass's findings in the ETS/LAUSD study. She also found no differences between computer and control groups in attitudes as measured by an Attitudes Toward Arithmetic Scale, or in times tardy to or absent from class.

Although the computer immersion treatment resulted in a comparatively large effect, Ferrell questioned the practical significance of this intensive computer use when weighed against the costs of implementation. She observed that "The practical magnitude of the differences was small, however, and coupled with other methodological problems.... The small differences obtained led to the conclusion that the computer immersion project did not demonstrate an impact even when time is maximized for any of the variables studied. School district officials concurred with this conclusion. The computer immersion model was dropped and the computers were put to other uses" (p. 335).

Minnesota Technology Demonstration Program

Morehouse, Hoaglund, and Schmidt (1987) reported disappointing results from a major two-year study of microcomputer use with Grade 4-6 students in

Minnesota schools. Over 20% of Minnesota school districts were involved and both microcomputer and video-based technologies were used. The computer-to-student ratio was very favorable and computer software was selected and used extensively and systematically based on skill needs. Morehouse et al. report that "virtually all of the large number of educators ...in this evaluation believe that technology, particularly computers, provides significant learning advantages" (p. 5).

In spite of these favorable conditions, Morehouse et al.'s (1987) results indicate that the average effect sizes achieved in mathematics, reading, and language were small negative ones (-.09 to -.31). The only area which showed positive results was that of improvements in writing skills through use of word processors. The report states that "The data suggest that some applications of technology, namely interactive television, do provide advantages.... The data do not indicate similar advantages--at least in terms of learning--of computers" (p. 5). These results indicate that computer-based methodologies, rather than helping students, may actually be hampering their learning in these key skill areas.

This report immediately came under fire from many instructional computing proponents who felt that computer use was not well-designed and carried out, and that the study was not controlled enough (Furor erupts, 1987). Criticisms of research methods do not appear to be valid in this case, and even if they were, could probably not account for the overall negative trend. Other studies, notably the Writing-to-Read project, had to be evaluated with little standard control over what went on in classrooms, and WTR still yielded overall positive effects. Instructional methods would seem to be a major source of the problems in this project. These results may serve as a warning to others thinking about large-scale computer implementation that teachers must be very clear on how technology is to be used, and measures of effectiveness must be closely tied to what is being taught in the courseware. It may also be that start-up problems with the program were later resolved and the usefulness of the program improved.

Logo Effects on Problem-solving Abilities: Pea's Bank Street Studies

Perhaps the most widely-publicized research on Logo effects was an extensive 18-month long study by Pea (1984) in which he examined the impact of Logo on planning skills. There were two different parts of the study: one in which Logo was taught through discovery learning methods, and the other where students learned Logo through directed instruction. Since Logo had been hypothesized to improve problem-solving abilities, Pea devised a task to measure planning skills, considered to be an important aspect of problem-solving. His attitude toward the possible effects of Logo was clear from his description of it in other papers (Pea, 1983). He refers to the belief that learning programming or any other activity can act as "wheaties of the mind," or a panacea for the problem of acquiring general thinking skills.

In the first part of the study, sixteen third and fifth grade students randomly assigned to the experimental group spent about 30 hours programming in Logo over the course of a year, and were encouraged to create their own Logo projects. An equal number of students in the control group received no problem-solving instruction. Planning efficiency, types of planning decisions, and decision flexibility were measured through an experimenter-designed rating system, while cognitive style was assessed through the WISC Block Design subtest. No significant differences were found between pre- and posttests of Logo and control groups on any of the measures. The effect size calculated on Pea's results was about .01.

In the second part of the study, thirty-two third and fifth grade students were again randomly assigned to a Logo or control group. This time, Logo instruction was more structured, and a modified version of the planning task was used. However, the results were the same. Virtually no treatment effects due to Logo could be found.

This study, like the one by Morehouse et al. (1987), was sharply criticized for its methods. In one of the most fascinating exchanges of opinions between academics ever published in the *Educational Researcher*, Papert (1987) and Pea (1987) defended their respective positions on the value of Logo and Logo research. Papert labeled the way in which Pea studied Logo as "technocentric," or attaching more importance to the computer and the programming language than the methods used with them. Pea replied that it was Papert, rather than he, who had originated the technocentric perspective, and that studying the effects of Logo uses is a legitimate and essential test. Pea also pointed out that the study was carried out by teachers who were initially enthusiastic about the discovery-learning method for learning Logo espoused by Papert, but who found that it was not feasible.

In addition to adding to the supplementary reading of computer-using educators, Pea's study and the published discussions which followed it served to demonstrate some important principles, all of which are echoed in the results of many other studies of computer applications. The first is that fervent belief in the value of technology is insufficient evidence of its value. As Kerlinger (1973) observed, "Strong subjective involvement is a powerful motivator for acquiring an objective approach to the study of phenomena" (p. vii). Second, the effectiveness of a given application depends very much on what measures are being used. Transfer of skills in the application to other, different skills in the posttest is rarely a good probability. Finally, the success of computer applications is always dependent on many other factors in addition to the design of the application itself: student characteristics, teacher methods, and the costs involved in the implementation.

SUMMARY FINDINGS
AND IMPLICATIONS

Literature on instructional computing after 1980 is replete with references to the "Microcomputer Revolution," implying that microcomputer applications have revolutionized classroom methods and greatly improved instructional effectiveness. While there is no doubt that education has changed dramatically as a result of microcomputer influence, the impact of applications of this technology on the traditional measures of instructional effectiveness (e.g., student achievement) has been difficult to measure. This review of studies published after 1980 and primarily from microcomputer uses is an attempt at estimating the impact of applications from the new era of technology on specific types of students, content, and skill areas. Also, since behavioral research is the only method of obtaining objective evidence on the effectiveness of instructional interventions of any kind, this review seeks to show the useful information provided by summarizing across studies using the new meta-analysis methods described. Hopefully, demonstrating the utility of this information will serve as a catalyst to individuals and agencies to support an increased level of research in the future.

The dissimilar study procedures and focuses which Slavin (1984) described about studies included in past meta-analyses were certainly present in the sample of studies in this review. While attempts were made to analyze across similar study characteristics and eliminate studies whose effects were dissimilar, the results of this review must still be viewed as very tentative.

The emphasis in the following sections is on showing the implications for future computer applications of research accomplished to date. To accomplish this goal, findings of research covered in this review will be compared with those of past reviews, both in terms of research procedures and focuses and in results. Even viewed within the limitations of meta-analysis procedures and the fewer-than-desirable number of studies, these findings provide much useful guidance to educators and decision-makers and to those planning to add to the body of research in this important area.

Comparison of Findings: Past and Present

Kulik (1987) found some 200 studies across all grade levels of his meta-analyses, which contained studies primarily from 1965 to 1980. In this review, the number of studies found from 1980 to 1987 was about 85. Of these, most were reported during the latter three years, indicating that instructional computing research may have dropped off slightly during the late 1970's and early 1980's, but is on the rise again. While this review served to confirm many of the findings of past reviews, there were also some dramatic differences between results from the two eras of technology.

Differences Between Past and Present Meta-analysis Procedures

To calculate study effect sizes for the current meta-analysis, similar methods were used as in past reviews of instructional computing research. Treatment effects are given in terms of standard deviation units and were corrected for sample size. However, instead of calculating product-moment correlations with study features, studies of similar characteristics such as content areas or grade levels were grouped together. The effect sizes in each of these groups was subjected to a statistical procedure called a test of homogeneity to determine if effects across studies were similar to each other. A 95% confidence interval was calculated for each effect size to indicate the range of effects into which the true effect might fall, since sampling error might make the true effect size more or less than the one reported. The computer program designed and written by the authors to accomplish this test calculated the following statistics:

1. Within group, between groups, and total homogeneity statistics (Q values) among studies
2. Effect sizes across studies (d+)
3. Effect sizes across groups in the analysis (d++)
4. Confidence intervals (95%) for each effect size
5. The value of Q contributed to the total group by a given study
6. The Q value remaining if a given study were to be deleted

If the Q value was significant at the .05 level, studies which were identified as outliers were deleted until the Q value was not significant and the analysis was re-done on the reduced set, resulting in adjusted effect sizes and confidence intervals. If several studies had to be deleted to achieve homogeneity, the set of outliers was analyzed informally to determine if there were common differences between the set and the rest of the studies which could account for the difference between them.

Trends in Research Topics and Characteristics

As was found in past reviews, most of the studies were in mathematics and reading, most of these were in basic skills, and about half of the total were from elementary grades. There was great variability among study features and procedures, and especially among the information given in the reports. Past reviewers usually note that, due to study flaws and lack of data, only a fraction of the total number of research reports available could be used. The current authors also encountered this problem and frequently had great difficulty determining just what had been done in the study, even how many subjects were in the experimental and control groups. Many studies had to be excluded because they did not provide standard deviation data or any other statistics from which effect sizes could be calculated.

Unlike Kulik's findings, the current review could identify no study features which were consistently associated with high or low effect sizes. The only exception to this trend was found in the comparison of computer applications for reading/language studies. In this analysis only, higher effects seemed to be associated with studies having non-computer control groups.

While studies in past reviews frequently measured learning retention and learning time, this study found little emphasis on these variables. Retention is a difficult factor to measure reliably, and researchers may be understandably reluctant to deal with its complexities. And, since most studies were in public schools which have a set time for grade levels and courses, it may be that decreasing learning time is not a practical concern. This review also found almost no studies on computer applications as a total replacement for traditional methods. Therefore, the variable of supplemental vs. replacement uses was not considered in this review. As was noted earlier in the summary of past reviews, computer applications seem destined as supplements to be integrated as appropriate into classroom instruction, rather than total systems of instruction in themselves.

The following observations can be made of research characteristics across studies in this review:

1. *Random Assignment* - Only about 40% of the achievement studies were able to accomplish that most desirable of research conditions: random assignment of students to experimental and control groups. Random assignment controls for many of the artifacts known to confound study results, but it is difficult to accomplish in field settings. Many of the researchers had to use intact classes of students rather than random assignment to groups, a much less satisfactory situation.

2. *Research designs* - Most studies that used random assignment also used pretest-posttest control group designs. Those which could not randomize used popular quasi-experimental methods such as matching subjects between groups, or letting students receiving one type of CAI control for those using CAI in another content area (e.g., measuring gains in mathematics and reading in the same study). Others used a non-equivalent pretest-posttest control group design.

3. *Computer control* - Although it is very helpful in controlling for Hawthorne effects, fewer than 30% of the studies had the control group use some

form of computer application. This is not surprising, since it is probably diffi-cult to get adequate access to computers for the experimental group, let alone the control group.

4. *Measures of achievement* - Researchers used a variety of tests, about 30% of which were locally-developed, almost always by the experimenter.(Re-liability was usually not reported.) Reading and mathematics studies often used subtests of the SRA, CTBS, ITBS, or CAT. Word processing studies most often used a wholistic scoring method designed by the experimenter. Where student attitudes or cognitive skills were being studied, no two experi-menters seemed to use the same instruments.

5. *Sample size* - The number of students in the study varied from a low of 16 to a high of about 4000. Most studies had a total N of around 100 stu-dents. Sample sizes were lower on the average in dissertation studies.

Trends in Study Results

The results of the analyses performed for this review are summarized in Table 23. The "% of Outliers" column shows the percentage of the studies re-quired to be omitted to achieve homogeneity of effects. The first column after that indicates whether or not the d resulting from the second analysis (after out-liers were omitted) is different from zero. The last column indicates whether or not d is the same among groups included in an analysis. Usually, achieving homogeneity within all groups in the analysis also removed the between groups variance. In the cases where groups were still significantly different from each other, the highest d is indicated with an "H."

As this Table indicates, positive effects which were significantly different from zero were found in every analysis except the ESL area, problem-solving CAI, achievement in females, and attitudes toward computers as instructional media. The small number of studies in all these analyses makes the findings suspect. However, the trends should not be ignored. The following compari-sons may be made between these results and those of past reviews:

1. *Attitudes* - In past reviews of attitudes, the most-studied variable seemed to be attitudes toward computers. This factor was not considered in this re-view, primarily because it was not felt to have important implications for stu-dents' learning. Of the variables considered, that of attitudes toward school and subject matter seemed most affected by computer use, and was also the most-studied. The effect was significantly different from zero, a result consis-tent with that of past reviews. Improving students' self-image and self-confidence through computer use, while a much-hypothesized and talked-about phenomenon, is still not much-studied. Only three studies with data were located which measured this variable, but the trend in these was consis-tently positive. Little data were also available on attitudes toward computers as

Table 23
Summary of Effect Sizes and Percentages of Outliers Across Groups

	Original Set d	Reduced Set d	% of Outliers	Different from 0*	Difference among groups**
ACHIEVEMENT:					
Elementary level	.32	.29	16%	*	*
Secondary level	.19	.19	14%	*	*
College/adult level	.57	.66	10%	*	* (H)
Mathematics	.36	.37	11%	*	
Science	.49	.64	25%	*	
Reading/language	.26	.30	27%	*	
Cognitive skills	.35	.28	7%	*	
Math drill/practice	.25	.20	6%	*	
Math tutorial	.22	.30	40%	*	
Math: Other applic's	.20	.38	13%	*	
Reading drill/practice	.26	.25	39%	*	
Reading tutorial	.41		0%	*	
Reading: Other applications	.32		0%	*	
Math computation	.24		0%	*	
Math concepts/PS	.26		0%	*	
Reading comprehension	.21		0%	*	
Reading vocabulary	.31	-.20	50%	*	
Reading word analysis	.55		0%	*	
Language usage/grammar	.30	.28	25%	*	
ESL	-.05	-.15	33%		
Word processing	.23		0%	*	
PS with Logo	.39		0%	*	* (H)
PS with CAI	.20	.01	25%		
Creativity	.73		0%	*	
Low-achieving students	.45	.36	7%	*	
Regular students	.32	.22	10%	*	
Females	.17	.12	9%		
Males	.19	.31	9%	*	
ATTITUDES:					
Self	.25		0%	*	
School/subject matter	.28		0%	*	
Computer medium	.06	.19	25%		
Females	.05	.18	20%	*	
Males	.29		0%	*	

* p<.05 that d is 0
** p<.05 that d is the same among groups (H=Highest d among groups)

instructional media, and resulting effects were not different from zero.

2. *Content area* - This review confirmed the trend in past studies that computer applications are more effective in teaching mathematics than reading/language skills. However, unlike past reviews, this study did not find significant differences between effects for reading and mathematics (p<.05). There was great variability among effects from reading studies, indicating that other factors accounted for differences among studies. Science achieved the highest overall effect size, but the small number of studies from this area limits the conclusions one may draw at this time. Perhaps most surprising was the finding that using computer applications to teach cognitive skills (problem-solving, critical thinking) yielded about the same effects as for reading and mathematics.

3. *Application type* - The only areas with sufficient numbers of studies to analyze in this way were reading and mathematics. Applications for mathematics seemed about equally effective. In reading, tutorial applications achieved higher effects than other types, a finding consistent with Roblyer and King's (1983) previous review of reading studies. However, effects among application types were not found to be significantly different (p<.05). While the trend seems to be that tutorials produce higher effects in reading, more studies need to be done in this area, particularly to address the question of whether or not drill seems more appropriate where lower-level skills are concerned (e.g., word analysis), and tutorials where higher level skills are being taught (e.g., comprehension). It should also be noted that the high positive effects from science studies were all with simulations for unstructured work. When drill software was used in science or when simulations were used for drill, much lower effects resulted. Clearly, the effectiveness of various types of CAI applications varies according to content area and skill being taught.

4. *Grade level* - The only significant differences among groups included in any analysis occurred in comparisons of elementary, secondary, and college levels. In marked contrast to past results which consistently found highest results at elementary levels, this review found significantly higher results at college/adult levels. Effects from elementary levels were higher than those at secondary levels, but differences were not very great. There were only half as many studies at the college level as at the secondary level, and only a quarter of the number for the elementary level. Still, the results indicate that, indeed, computer applications can be as successful at higher levels, and may be even more effective than at lower levels.

5. *Types of students* - Although findings in Table 23 appear to indicate greater effectiveness of computer applications with lower-achieving students than with regular, on-grade students, this difference in effects was actually not significant. It should be noted in this summary as it was in the summary of past reviews that software especially designed for slow learners may be more

effective with them than software designed for the general population. The findings of the large-scale ETS study of Writing to Read may be an indication of this trend, since the program was designed for the general population, but was actually considerably less successful with minority and disadvantaged learners. There were no significant differences between males and females in achievement with computer-based methods, but the inconclusive nature of the data points out the need for careful attention to this area. Finally, there was a clear indication, based on only a few studies, that computer-based instruction with Spanish-speaking populations may not be as effective as other methods.

Implications of Findings for Future Research

One need only look at the useful information provided by summarized research and the small number of studies available at this time in many key areas to conclude that an increased level of research in instructional computing is important to the field. The results of the present review, based on only a relatively few studies, has indicated some areas in which computer applications are more effective than others and some where they are apparently not effective at all. Yet other factors could be at work in the sampling of studies, and further investigation of the true causes of these differences is needed. In considering the work which must be done in the future, the following concerns arise.

Recognizing the Need for Research

While there is apparently a resurgence in computer applications studies after a lull in pre-microcomputer years, research is clearly not the priority it should be in this field. The budget for research and evaluation is small in comparison to that for hardware, and there are few agencies which gather evidence of technology's effectiveness as part of their on-going mission. In the clamor created by claims and counter-claims about computer effects on learning, the unemotional voice of scientific inquiry is a valuable arbiter. It seems singularly unproductive to accept the beliefs of the committed at face value, or to take the position that the true merits of computer usage cannot be measured. Nor are unsystematic observations and anecdotal evidence sufficient to guide decision-makers in allocating funds for computer resources. For those who wish to see the field develop its full potential for improving teaching and learning, it is a time for "back to basics"--basic questions about the effects of computer applications and basic research to address these questions.

Most pertinent to today's problems are the observations of Campbell and Stanley from that most basic of all research texts, *Experimental and Quasi-Experimental Designs for Research* (1963). In stating their commitment to experimental research, they identify it as "the only means for settling disputes regarding educational practice, as the only way of verifying educational improvements, and as the only way of establishing a cumulative tradition in which improvements can be introduced without the danger of a faddish discard of old wisdom in favor of inferior novelties" (p. 2). While they acknowledge that the results of individual experiments can be disappointing, they justify continued research on the grounds that it is "not a panacea, but rather the only available route to cumulative progress" (p. 3).

The concept of cumulative progress is an important one. One study, no matter how large or comprehensive, is not as important as evidence gathered over time as experimenters learn more and more about the questions to ask and the ways to structure appropriate research in a given area. An on-going commitment both to support and use the results of systematic study is necessary. In order to accomplish this, perceptions about the value of behavioral research must change in several ways:

• Educational organizations must change their perspectives on research, accept it as a requirement for development and growth, and give it a funding priority along with hardware and software.

• Funding agencies must accept the need for more and better research in instructional computing methods, provide the funds to support it, and solicit on-going research projects to answer key questions.

• Practitioners must begin to rely on the results of research to indicate the validity of their beliefs and hypotheses, and insist that their organizations provide the data which are needed.

Developing this kind of support for research would benefit all areas of educational practice. It would also begin to build the knowledge base which has been lacking for so long in education.

Specific Areas of Needed Research

The results of this review indicate several areas of research which are in urgent need of further information and explication. Some of these areas were described previously in a summary on research needs by Roblyer (1985b) and seem even more important in light of current results. The following may be of particular interest to doctoral students searching for a dissertation question:

1. *Applications in various skill and content areas* - While there seem to be differences in effects of computer applications among content areas, these differences may be due to the type of application interacting with the type of skill within the content area. The following represent only a few of the important areas requiring further study:

-Measuring effects of a specific kind of application designed to teach one type of mathematics or reading skill

-Comparing effects of a specific kind of application designed to teach two or more types of reading skills

-Comparing effects of similar programs from the same developer on the same level of mathematics vs. reading skills (e.g., computations and word analysis skills)

-Measuring effects of science applications (and ways of using them)

-Comparing effects of a specific kind of application (e.g., simulations) on lower level vs. higher level skills

2. *Computer applications in ESL* - In light of the low effects to date in this area, further evaluations are needed of existing computer packages for ESL students. Comparisons of Hispanic students in computer and non-computer instructional programs is essential.

3. *Word processing use* - While effects seem small at this time in this area, more work must be done on ways of maximizing effects on quality of students' written work. More studies also need to focus on measuring attitudes toward writing as a result of word processing and the impact of these attitudes on how much students actually write.

4. *Creativity and problem-solving with Logo and CAI* - While results of Logo applications seem promising and those for unstructured CAI are disappointing, further study must be directed toward areas such as the following:

-Comparing effects of Logo vs. well-designed non-computer instructional programs on problem-solving and creativity

-Measuring effects of Logo use on general problem-solving abilities

-Evaluating the effects of various teaching methods and learning methods (e.g., discovery vs. structured) with Logo

-Measuring the transfer of Logo-developed problem-solving abilities to specific content area problem-solving skills

-Measuring the impact of CAI software specifically designed to improve problem-solving and creative abilities

-Measuring and comparing the effects of Logo usage on students with various characteristics (e.g., learning styles, intelligence levels)

5. *Effects of computer use on attitudes and drop-out rate* - Results of studies which presented statistical data indicate that computer use has a positive impact on students' attitudes toward school and learning. Since so few studies with data were located which measured student preferences for computer media and the impact on students' self-concept of using computer applications, results are unclear in this area. More data must be gathered on the following:

-Further evidence of changes in self-concept and in student attitudes toward subject matter, and factors which most affect these attitudes

-Evidence of preferences for computer-based media over other media

-The impact of improved attitudes on decreases in drop-out behavior

6. *Effects of computer use on achievement of males vs. females* - The inconclusive nature of available data make this a vital topic for future work.

More Cost-Effectiveness Studies

In a recent concise and well-written summary of an earlier, more lengthy report, Levin and Meister (1986) discussed the results of a recent study comparing the costs and effects of CAI with three other types of interventions: cross-age tutoring, increasing instructional time, and reducing class size. Their conclusion was that CAI, while effective in teaching elementary mathematics and reading, was not as cost-effective as peer tutoring.

While this study came under immediate criticism from CAI-proponents (Niemiec, Blackwell, and Walberg, 1986), the authenticity of the issues raised by cost-effectiveness experts like Levin and Meister cannot be denied. Clearly, more work must be done on cost-effectiveness, particularly since the study used by Levin's team to estimate effects was the ETS/LAUSD study, using mainframe technology and older software. While Levin's team chose this study because it was the most well-designed research available on perhaps the most well-known of CAI systems, better effects may have been found with another well-designed study on newer technology and software, e.g., Project IMPAC. The methods and measures used by Levin et al. would seem excellent tools to complete such studies.

Standards for Research Reports

Few activities are as difficult to do well as experimental research. Accomplishing this feat is a singular achievement. But no matter what the purpose or result of a research study, its importance is doubled if the findings are able to be added to the body of evidence in the area. As the *Publication Manual* for the American Psychological Association (1983) states, "Research is complete only when the results are shared with the scientific community" (p. 17). But not only should a study be reported clearly and completely, so that readers can understand its procedures and interpret its results, the report should contain sufficient information to allow it to be compared with other studies and included in summaries of research in the area. Also, clear, comprehensive reports are necessary for replication and for follow-up studies. Only then can the concept of cumulative progress through research become feasible.

Many of the studies considered for this review could not be included because they failed to report basic descriptive data. Others are limited in their usefulness because they give insufficient detail on their research procedures and statistical methods. Standards in research reporting of the kind described in the *APA Publication Manual* would have obvious benefit for future research and reviews of research in instructional computing. If experimenters would observe the following rules for reporting, it would be especially helpful to those attempting to summarize across studies with a meta-analysis procedure:

• *Statistical data* - Descriptive statistics, especially means and standard deviations, should always be reported along with inferential statistics such as significance of t-tests or F-ratios from ANOVA's. If possible, means and standard deviations should be reported for both pretests and posttests and for all subgroups (e.g., males and females, Hispanics and Anglos, low achievers and high achievers) in the total sample. Include results for both dependent variables which were significant and those which failed to achieve significance, and give the values, degrees of freedom, and probability level of each.

• *Sample sizes* - Give the number of subjects in both the experimental (E) and control groups (C), and in the E and C groups for each subgroup in the sample (e.g., males in each E and C and females in each E and C). Be sure to indicate any attrition of subjects which occurred between the initial selection of subjects and the final posttesting.

• *Test instrument information* - The instrument used to measure each variable should be described along with its reliability. For example, if a test of creativity is used, a brief description of the activity required in the test would be helpful.

• *Treatment information* - Supply information on what the control group did during the study, as well as what the experimental group did. In addition to indicating that the control group got "traditional math instruction," indicate what activities that entailed. The amount of time spent on each kind of activity is an important variable, and descriptions should include how much time was spent during each session, how many sessions per week or month, and how many total weeks or months elapsed between pretest and posttest.

• *Design information* - Include a clear description of the study's design using traditional terminology. For example, indicate if the study had a pretest-posttest design, non-equivalent control group design, or other procedure to structure the study. State clearly if subjects were randomly assigned or if intact classes were assigned to treatments.

These items of information should be required in every research report. Reviewers for journals should strive to assure that these minimum standards are met in every article accepted for publication. Of course, the importance of clear, concise written summaries of study procedures and results cannot be over-emphasized. Researchers would do well to give their written summaries to at least one other research expert and at least one district-level evaluation expert and ask them if the purpose, procedures, results, and implications of the study are clear to them from the report.

Implications of Findings for Future Implementation

To have any meaning for education, research results must be related to what

sions at this time. Providing laboratory experiences with computer simulations may be an especially powerful method in higher level lab work in science. There are indications that this may be one of the few skill areas in which computer use can do what no other medium can do, and, if used correctly (as tools to analyze information), can also yield better results than any other instructional method. Mathematics and science areas consistently yield higher effect sizes than reading and cognitive skill applications, but the results within these latter areas vary dramatically. To determine the most appropriate uses of computer applications for reading and cognitive skill instruction, one must look to the kinds of skills and applications. No decision can be made across a content area without more specific information on how computers are being used.

3. *Computer use by skill area* - All levels of skills in reading and mathematics should be expected to profit from computer-based methods, but the kind of application seems to make a dramatic difference in some areas. In reading, the trend indicates that computer applications should be most effective in teaching lower-level word analysis skills and least effective in teaching higher-level comprehension skills. Word processing with writing skills can be recommended, not only in light of educationally significant effects and the fact that students seem to feel more positively about writing when using these tools, but also because it makes writing a physically easier activity. All types of applications should be equally effective in mathematics, while tutorials can be expected to be generally more effective than other applications in reading areas. In cognitive skills, using Logo as a method of teaching reasoning and problem solving skills should be effective, but use of unstructured CAI should be viewed with caution unless it is implemented with very different instructional methods from those documented in past studies.

4. *Computer use with student groups* - Computer applications can be about equally effective with low-achieving and regular students. Since there is no firm evidence of achievement differences between males and females, no changes to current implementation can be recommended at this time. Special caution should be used, however, when using computers to teach English or reading as a second language with Hispanic students, since results indicate that these applications may be less effective than non-computer methods. Again, modifying the kind of instructional approach from that used in the past may make a difference in the impact of ESL computer applications.

5. *Shaping attitudes through computer use* - Even though uses of computers should have a positive impact on students' attitudes toward themselves and their subject matter, educators should not expect to justify the purchase or use of computer systems by effects on attitudes. This is especially true since no relationship has been established between attitudes toward computers and achievement. Results are simply not that convincing to date that students are more motivated by computers, and the relationship of student attitudes to

achievement and to decreasing drop-out rate remains unknown.

Administrators contemplating a computer-based package for system-wide use in such basic areas as reading or mathematics should consider not only effect sizes but cost-effectiveness as well. The best evidence to date is that large scale use of a computer system for basic skills instruction will not be as cost-effective as non-computer ones such as peer tutoring. Unless the computer hardware and software can be used for a variety of other applications at the same time, it will be difficult to justify costs of purchasing, planning for, and maintaining the system. Making sure of the following may help improve the results from such systems:

-The skills addressed in the software are the specific ones being measured in the posttests.

-Courseware is especially designed for the needs of the target students.

-The system is the lowest-cost one available (both in terms of start-up and maintenance) which has evidence of effectiveness.

A Final Word on the Future

Revolutions have a way of mandating change while glossing over logistical details of how to implement that change, and such has certainly been the case with the "Microcomputer Revolution" in education during the last ten years. Research is the tool which can help make sure the revolution has practical implications for schools. The results of this review have indicated clearly that more is not necessarily better; newer, not always an improvement. The findings have also made it clear that computer applications have an undeniable value and an important instructional role to play in classrooms in the future. Defining that role is the task of the next decade.

There is, of course, never a final word on the future; it is always before us. But the opportunity now before us will not always be there. Educators are currently enthusiastic and supportive of computer-assisted instruction, computer-based discovery-learning materials, and computer productivity tools. But that enthusiasm will wane, as it does with all new things. Unless a clear case can be made soon with research and evaluation results for keeping a computer application in use, it may be one of the methods "in danger of faddish discard" of which Campbell and Stanley (1963) warned. This review has shown that that would indeed be a loss. Opportunities for making technology have an impact on education have never been greater--and neither have opportunities for research in instructional computing. The next decade must be a time for taking full advantage of both.

REFERENCES

Past Reviews

Aiello, N. C., & Wolfle, L. M. (1980, April). *A meta-analysis of individualized instruction in science*. Paper presented at the annual meeting of the American Educational Research Association, Boston, MA. (ERIC Document Reproduction Service No. ED 190 404)

Bangert-Drowns, R. L., Kulik, J. A., & Kulik, C. C. (1985). Effectiveness of computer-based education in secondary schools. *Journal of Computer-Based Instruction*, 12, 59-68.

Blume, G. W. (1984, April). *A review of research on the effects of computer programming on mathematical problem solving*. Paper presented at the annual meeting of the American Educational Research Association, New Orleans, LA.

Burns, P. K., & Bozeman, W. C. (1981, October). Computer-assisted instruction and mathematics achievement: Is there a relationship? *Educational Technology*, 21 (10), 32-39.

Carter, J. (1984). Instructional learner feedback: A literature review with implications for software development. *The Computing Teacher*, 12(2), 53-55.

Cohen, J. (1977). *Statistical power analysis for the behavioral sciences* (Rev. ed.). New York: Academic Press.

Crosby, H. M. (1983). *The effectiveness of the instructional use of computers for students with mild learning problems: A review of the literature and research* (Concepts and issues paper, University of Illinois at Urbana-Champaign). (ERIC Document Reproduction Service No. ED 249 688)

Edwards, J., Norton, S., Taylor, S., Weiss, M., & Dusseldorp, R. (1975, November). How effective is CAI? A review of the research. *Educational Leadership*, 33(2), 147-153.

Florida Department of Education. (1980). *More hands for teachers: Report of the Commisioner's Advisory Committee on Instructional Computing*. Tallahassee, FL: Office of Educational Technology.

Glass, G. V (1976). Primary, secondary, and meta-analysis of research. *Educational Researcher*, 5, 3-8.

Glass, G. V (1977). Integrating findings: The meta-analysis of research. In L. Shulman (Ed.), *Review of research in education*. Itasca, IL: Peacock.

Glass, G. V (1982). Assessment of the effectiveness of computer-assisted instruction in the ETS-Los Angeles study. In M. Ragosta, P. W. Holland, & D. T. Jamison (Eds.), *Computer-assisted instruction and compensatory education: The ETS/LAUSD study*. Princeton, NJ: Educational Testing Service.

REFERENCES: Past Reviews (continued)

Hasselbring, T. S. (1984, July). *Research on the effectiveness of computer-based instruction: A review.* Nashville, TN: The Learning Technology Center, George Peabody College of Vanderbilt University. (ERIC Document Reproduction Service No. ED 262 754)

Hasselbring, T. S. (1987). Effective computer use in special education: What does the research tell us? In *Effectiveness of microcomputers in education* (Funder Forum, pp. 23-41). Cupertino, CA: Apple Computer, Inc.

Hathaway, M. D. (1984, January). Variables of computer screen display and how they affect learning. *Educational Technology*, 24(1), 7-11.

Hawisher, G. E. (1986). Studies in word processing. *Computers and Composition*, 4 (1), 8-31.

Hunter, B. (1987). Computer-based tools in learning and teaching: A research agenda. In *Effectiveness of microcomputers in education* (Funder Forum, pp. 77-122). Cupertino, CA: Apple Computer, Inc.

Jamison, D., Suppes, P., & Wells, S. (1974). The effectiveness of alternative instructional media: A survey. *Review of Educational Research*, 44(1), 1-67.

Kulik, C. C., Kulik, J. A., & Schwalb, B. J. (1986). Effectiveness of computer-based adult education: A meta-analysis. *Journal of Educational Computing Research*, 2, 235-252.

Kulik, J. A. (1981, April). *Integrating findings from different levels of instruction.* Paper presented at the annual meeting of the American Educational Research Association, Los Angeles, CA.

Kulik, J. A. (1985, April). *Consistencies in findings on computer-based education.* Paper presented at the annual meeting of the American Educational Research Association, Chicago, IL.

Kulik, J. A., Bangert, R. L., & Williams, G. W. (1983). Effects of computer-based teaching on secondary school students. *Journal of Educational Psychology*, 75(1), 19-26.

Kulik, J. A., & Bangert-Drowns, R. L. (1983-84). Effectiveness of technology in precollege mathematics and science teaching. *Journal of Educational Technology Systems*, 12(2), 137-158.

Kulik, J. A., & Kulik, C. C. (1987). Review of recent research literature on computer-based instruction. *Contemporary Educational Psychology*, 12, 222-230.

Kulik, J. A., Kulik, C. C., & Bangert-Drowns, R. L. (1985). Effectiveness of computer-based education in elementary schools. *Computers in Human Behavior*, 1, 59-74.

Kulik, J. A., Kulik, C. C., & Cohen, P. A. (1980). Effectiveness of computer-based college teaching: A meta-analysis of findings. *Review of Educational Research*, 50(4), 525-544.

REFERENCES: Past Reviews (continued)

Lawton, J., & Gerschner, V. T. (1982). A review of the literature on attitudes towards computers and computerized instruction. *Journal of Research and Development in Education,* 16(1), 50-55.

Levin, H. M. (1985). Costs and cost-effectiveness of computer-assisted instruction. *Public Budgeting & Finance,* 5(1), 27-42.

Levin, H. M., Glass, G. V, & Meister, G. (1986). The political arithmetic of cost-effectiveness analysis. *Phi Delta Kappan,* 68, 69-72.

Levin, H. M., & Meister, G. (1986). Is CAI cost-effective? *Phi Delta Kappan,* 67, 745-749.

Niemiec, R., Samson, G., Weinstein, T., & Walberg, H. J. (1987). The effects of computer based instruction in elementary schools: A quantitative synthesis. *Journal of Research on Computing in Education,* 20(2), 85-103.

Niemiec, R. P., & Walberg, H. J. (1985). Computers and achievement in the elementary schools. *Journal of Educational Computing Research,* 1(4), 435-440.

Okey, J. R. (1985, April). *The effectiveness of computer-based education: A review.* Paper presented at the annual meeting of the National Association for Research in Science Teaching, French Lick Springs, IN. (ERIC Document Reproduction Service No. ED 257 677)

Orlansky, J. (1983). Effectiveness of CAI: A different finding. *Electronic Learning,* 3(1), 58, 60.

Roblyer, M. D. (1985a). *Measuring the impact of computers in instruction: A non-technical review of research for educators.* Washington, DC: The Association for Educational Data Systems.

Roblyer, M. D., & King, F. J. (1983). *Reasonable expectations for computer-based instruction in basic reading skills.* Paper presented at the annual conference of the Association for Educational Communications and Technology, New Orleans, LA.

Samson, G. E., Niemiec, R., Weinstein, T., & Walberg, H. J. (1985, April). *Effects of computer-based instruction on secondary school achievement: A quantitative synthesis.* Paper presented at the annual meeting of the American Educational Research Association, Chicago, IL.

Stennett, R. G. (1985). *Computer assisted instruction: A review of the reviews.* London, Ontario: The Board of Education for the City of London. (ERIC Document Reproduction Service No. ED 260 687)

Thomas, D. B. (1979, Spring). The effectiveness of computer-assisted instruction in secondary schools. *AEDS Journal,* pp. 103-116.

Vinsonhaler, J. F., & Bass, R. K. (1972, July). A summary of ten major studies on CAI drill and practice. *Educational Technology,* pp. 29-32.

Willett, J. B., Yamashita, J. M., & Anderson, R. D. (1983). A meta-analysis of instructional systems applied in science teaching. *Journal of Research in Science Teaching,* 20(5), 405-417.

REFERENCES:
Achievement Meta-analyses

Alessi, S. M., Siegel, M., Silver, D., & Barnes, H. (1982). Effectiveness of a computer-based reading comprehension program for adults. *Journal of Educational Technology Systems*, 1(1), 43-57.

Battista, M. T., & Clements, D. H. (1986). The effects of Logo and CAI problem-solving environments on problem-solving abilities and mathematics achievement. *Computers in Human Behavior*, 2, 183-193.

Berlin, D. F., & White, A. L. (1985, March). The computer as transition from object manipulation to abstract visuo-spatial thought. *International Conference Proceedings of the Association for the Development of Computer-Based Instructional Systems* (Philadelphia, PA), pp. 222-229. (ERIC Document Reproduction Service No. ED 258 561)

Carrier, C., Post, T. R., & Heck, W. (1985). Using microcomputers with fourth-grade students to reinforce arithmetic skills. *Journal of Research in Mathematics Education*, 16(1), 45-51.

Clements, D. H., & Gullo, D. F. (1984). Effects of computer programming on young children's cognition. *Journal of Educational Psychology*, 76(6), 1051-1058.

Degelman, D., Free, J. U., Scarlato, M., Blackburn, J. M., & Golden, T. (1986). Concept learning in preschool children: Effects of a short-term Logo experience. *Journal of Educational Computing Research*, 2(2), 199-205.

Ferrell, B. G. (1986). Evaluating the impact of CAI on mathematics learning: Computer immersion project. *Journal of Educational Computing Research*, 2(3), 327-336.

Fortner, R. W., Schar, & Mayer, V. J. (1986). *Effect of microcomputer simulations on computer awareness and perception of environmental relationships among college students*. Columbus, OH: Ohio State University, Office of Learning Resources. (ERIC Document Reproduction Service No. ED 270 311)

Goodwin, L. D., Goodwin, W. L., Nansel, A., & Helm, C. P. (1986). Cognitive and affective effects of various types of microcomputer use by preschoolers. *American Educational Research Journal*, 23(3), 348-356.

Hawisher, G. E. (1986, April). *The effects of word processing on the revision strategies of college students*. Paper presented at the annual meeting of the American Educational Research Association, San Francisco, CA. (ERIC Document Reproduction Service No. ED 268 546)

Hawley, D. E., Fletcher, J. D., & Piele, P. K. (1986, November). *Costs, effects, and utility of microcomputer-assisted instruction*. Eugene, OR: University of Oregon,

REFERENCES: Achievement Meta-analyses (continued)

Center for Advanced Technology in Education.

Henderson, R. W., Landesman, E. M., & Kachuck, I. (1985). Computer-video instruction in mathematics: Field test of an interactive approach. *Journal of Research in Mathematics Education,* 16(3), 207-224.

Horton, J., & Ryba, K. (1986, August/September). Assessing learning with Logo: A pilot study. *The Computing Teacher,* pp. 24-28.

Kerchner, L. B., & Kistinger, B. J. (1984). Language processing/word processing: Written expression, computers and learning disabled students. *Learning Disability Quarterly,* 7, 329-335.

Kraus, W. H. (1981). Using a computer game to reinforce skills in addition basic facts in second grade. *Journal of Research in Mathematics Education,* 12(2), 152-155.

Kurth, R. J. (1987, January). Using word processing to enhance revision strategies during student writing activities. *Educational Technology,* pp. 13-19.

Lavin, R. J., & Sanders, J. E. (1983, April). *Longitudinal evaluation of the computer assisted instruction Title I project.* Chelmsford, MA: Metrics Associates, Inc. (ERIC Document Reproduction Service No. ED 234 119)

Leigh, R. K., Horn, C. J. Jr., & Campbell, D. L. (1984, November). *A comparison of third grade student performance in division of whole numbers using a microcomputer drill program and a print drill program.* Paper presented at the Annual Mid-South Educational Research Conference, New Orleans, LA. (ERIC Document Reproduction Service No. ED 253 431)

Massey, C., & Gelormino, J. (1987, April). *The influence of a math software program on preschoolers' acquisition of mathematics: Ruton in the classroom.* Paper presented at the annual meeting of the American Educational Research Association, Washington, DC.

McDermott, C. W. (1985, December). *Affecting basic skills achievement through technology: A research report.* Little Rock: Arkansas State Department of Education.

Millar, G., & MacLeod, A. (1984, September). *Microcomputer learning project.* Claresholm, Alberta: Willow Creek School Division No. 28.

Moore, C., Smith, S., & Avner, R. A. (1980). Facilitation of laboratory performance through CAI. *Journal of Chemical Education,* 57(3), 196-198.

Morehouse, D. L., Hoaglund, M. L., & Schmidt, R. H. (1987, February). *Technology demonstration program final evaluation report.* Menomonie, WI: Quality Evaluation & Development.

Murphy, R. T., & Appel, L. R. (1984, November). *Evaluation of the Writing to Read instructional system, 1982-1984:   A presentation from the second year report.* Princeton, NJ: Educational Testing Service.

Pea, R. D., & Kurland, D. M. (1984, March). *Logo programming and the development of planning skills* (Technical Report No. 16). New York: Bank Street College of

REFERENCES: Achievement Meta-analyses (continued)

Education.

Perkins, H. W., & Bass, G. M. (1984, June). *The effects of microcomputer use on the teaching of critical thinking skills to middle school students.* Paper presented at the National Educational Computing Conference, Dayton, OH.

Piel, J. A., & Baller, W. A. (1986). Effects of computer assistance on acquisition of Piagetian conceptualization among children of ages two to four. *AEDS Journal,* 19(2-3), 210-215.

Reid, E. R., Collett, M. F., & Parker, E. C. (1986). *Keyboarding, reading, spelling (KRS).* Salt Lake City, UT: Reid Foundation.

Reimer, G. (1985, January/February). The effects of a Logo computer programming experience on readiness for first grade, creativity, and self concept. "A pilot study in kindergarten." *AEDS Monitor,* pp. 8-12.

Rieber, L. P. (1987, February). Logo and its promise: A research report. *Educational Technology,* pp. 12-16.

Saracho, O. N. (1982). The effects of a computer-assisted instruction program on basic skills achievement and attitudes toward instruction of Spanish-speaking migrant children. *American Educational Research Journal,* 19(2), 201-219.

Schaeffer, R. H. (1981). Meaningful practice on the computer: Is it possible? *Foreign Language Annals,* 14(2), 133-137.

Wainwright, C. L. (1985, April). *The effectiveness of a computer-assisted instruction package in supplementing teaching of selected concepts in high school chemistry: Writing formulas and balancing chemical equations.* Paper presented at the annual meeting of the National Association for Research in Science Teaching, French Lick Springs, IN. (ERIC Document Reproduction Service No. ED 257 656)

Waldron, M. B. (1985). A computer graphics tutorial to teach orthographic projection. *Engineering Education,* 75(4), 237-239.

Watkins, M. W., & Abram, S. (1985, April). Reading CAI with first grade students. *The Computing Teacher,* 12(7), 43-45.

REFERENCES:
Dissertation Studies

Abram, S. L. (1984). The effect of computer assisted instruction on first grade phonics and mathematics. *Dissertation Abstracts International,* 45(4), 1032A. (University Microfilms No. 84-16161)

Ash, R. C. (1985). An analysis of the cost-effectiveness of a computer-assisted instructional program. *Dissertation Abstracts International,* 47(8), 2137A. (University Microfilms No. 85-23784)

Bamberger, H. J. (1984). The effect of Logo (turtle graphics) on the problem solving strategies used by fourth grade children. *Dissertation Abstracts International,* 46(4), 918A. (University Microfilms No. 85-12171)

Bryg, V. (1984). The effect of computer-assisted instruction upon reading achievement with selected fourth-grade children. *Dissertation Abstracts International,* 45(9), 2817A. (University Microfilms No. 84-27899)

Cheever, M. S. (1987). The effects of using a word processor on the acquisition of composition skills by the elementary student (Doctoral dissertation, Northwestern University, 1987).

Coomes, P. A. (1985). The effects of computer assisted instruction on the development of reading and language skills. *Dissertation Abstracts International,* 46(11), 3302A. (University Microfilms No. 85-27359)

Cooperman, K. S. (1985). An experimental study to compare the effectiveness of a regular classroom reading program to a regular classroom reading program with a CAI program in reading comprehension skills in grades 2-4. *Dissertation Abstracts International,* 46(5), 1234A. (University Microfilms No. 85-15764)

Crawford, V. F. (1984). A comparison study of computer-assisted instruction and traditional classroom instruction in selected units of a college business mathematics course. *Dissertation Abstracts International,* 45(11), 3333A. (University Microfilms No. 85-00163)

Darling, D. L. (1986). A study of the effects using microcomputers on achievement in mathematics basic skills. *Dissertation Abstracts International,* 47(3), 785A. (University Microfilms No. 86-11590)

Davidson, R. L. (1986). The effectiveness of computer assisted instruction of Chapter I students in secondary schools. *Dissertation Abstracts International,* 47(2), 399A. (University Microfilms No. 86-08257)

Dyarmett, C. J. (1986). The influence of computer-assisted instruction versus traditional instruction on the academic achievement of high school students enrolled in beginning accounting courses. *Dissertation Abstracts International,*

141

REFERENCES: Dissertation Studies (continued)

47(8), 2819A. (University Microfilms No. 86-26445)

Easterling, B. A. (1983). The effects of computer assisted instruction as a supplement to classroom instruction in reading comprehension and arithmetic. *Dissertation Abstracts International*, 43(7), 2231A. (University Microfilms No. 82-28032)

Elliott, E. L. (1986). The effects of computer-assisted instruction upon the basic skill proficiencies of secondary vocational education students. *Dissertation Abstracts International*, 46(11), 3329A. (University Microfilms No. 86-00439)

Englebert, B. B. (1983). A study of the effectiveness of microcomputer-assisted math instruction on the achievement of selected secondary SLD students. *Dissertation Abstracts International*, 45(3), 737A. (University Microfilms No. 84-14911)

Feldhausen, M. W. (1986). The effects of computer review assistance modules (CRAM) on student achievement in U. S. history. *Dissertation Abstracts International*, 47(1), 68A. (University Microfilms No. 86-06961)

Fickel, M. G. (1986). The effects of Logo study on problem-solving cognitive abilities of sixth-grade students. *Dissertation Abstracts International*, 47(6), 2066A. (University Microfilms No. 86-14452)

Forte, M. M. (1984). The effects of a 'Logo' computer program versus a 'mathematics' computer program on reflection-impulsivity, perceived competence, motivational orientation, and academic achievement. *Dissertation Abstracts International*, 45(9), 2803A. (University Microfilms No. 84-28718)

Hamby, C. S. (1985). A study of the effects of computer-assisted instruction on the attitude and achievement of vocational nursing students. *Dissertation Abstracts International*, 46(10), 2904A. (University Microfilms No. 85-28326)

Hoffman, J. T. (1984). Reading achievement and attitude toward reading of elementary students receiving supplementary CAI compared with students receiving supplementary traditional instruction. *Dissertation Abstracts International*, 45(7), 2050A. (University Microfilms No. 84-23032)

Kaczor, C. T. (1986). Academic achievement of agricultural mechanics students using computer-assisted versus written review and testing. *Dissertation Abstracts International*, 47(7), 2424A. (University Microfilms No. 86-23337)

Kochinski, V. A. (1986). The effect of CAI for remediation on the self-concepts, attitudes, and reading achievement of middle school readers. *Dissertation Abstracts International*, 47(6), 2100A. (University Microfilms No. 86-20302)

Levy, M. H. (1985). An evaluation of computer assisted instruction upon the achievement of fifth grade students as measured by standardized tests. *Dissertation Abstracts International*, 46(4), 860A. (University Microfilms No. 85-13059)

Lewinter, B. W. (1986). A study of the influence of Logo on locus of control,

REFERENCES: Dissertation Studies (continued)

attitudes toward mathematics, and problem-solving ability in children in grades 4, 5, 6. *Dissertation Abstracts International*, 47(5), 1640. (University Microfilms No. 86-16959)

Mann, R. J. (1986). The effects of Logo computer programming on problem solving abilities of eighth grade students. *Dissertation Abstracts International*, 47(5), 1702A. (University Microfilms No. 86-19040)

Mason, M. M. (1984). A longitudinal study of the effects of computer assisted instruction on the mathematics achievement of the learning disabled and educable mentally retarded. *Dissertation Abstracts International*, 45(9), 2791. (University Microfilms No. 84-28270)

McCormack, S. K. (1986). The effect of computer assisted instruction on letter-sound recognition and beginning reading skills for kindergarten students. *Dissertation Abstracts International*, 47(3), 839A. (University Microfilms No. 86-08625)

Melnik, L. (1986). Investigation of two methods for improving problem-solving performance of fifth grade students. *Dissertation Abstracts International*, 47(2), 405A. (University Microfilms No. 86-05549)

Meyer, P. A. (1986). A comparative analysis of the value of intrinsic motivation in computer software on the math achievement, attitudes, attendance, and depth-of-involvement of underachieving students. *Dissertation Abstracts International*, 47(4), 1295A. (University Microfilms No. 86-13994)

Miller, S. (1984). A comparison of computer-assisted instruction with prescription learning and the traditional "pull-out" program used in supplementing instruction of mathematics basic skills to chapter I students. *Dissertation Abstracts International*, 44(08), 2397A. (University Microfilms No. 83-26453)

Millman, P. G. (1984). The effects of computer-assisted instruction on attention deficits, achievement, and attitudes of learning disabled children. *Dissertation Abstracts International*, 45(10), 3114A. (University Microfilms No. 84-2489)

Noda, P. C. (1983). Exploratory study of the impact of computer-assisted instruction on the English language reading achievement of LEP Arabic and Chaldean middle school students. *Dissertation Abstracts International*, 44(12), 3590A. (University Microfilms No. 84-06002)

Ojeda, E. (1984). Effectiveness of a computer assisted instruction supported bilingual program for Hispanic students. *Dissertation Abstracts International*, 45 (3), 740A. (University Microfilms No. 84-14520)

Olson, J. K. (1986). Using Logo to supplement the teaching of geometric concepts in the elementary school classroom. *Dissertation Abstracts International*, 47(3), 819A. (University Microfilms No. 86-11553)

Ortmann, L. N. (1984). The effectiveness of supplementary computer-assisted

REFERENCES: Dissertation Studies (continued)

instruction in reading at the 4-6 grade level. *Dissertation Abstracts International,* 45(1), 140A. (University Microfilms No. 84-08204)

Pivarnik, B. A. (1985). The effect of training in word processing on the writing quality of 11th grade students. *Dissertation Abstracts International,* 46(7), 1827A. (University Microfilms No. 85-20666)

Reid, M. N. (1986). A comparative study of three teaching methods used in adult basic education and general educational development mathematics programs. *Dissertation Abstracts International,* 47(8), 2853A. (University Microfilms No. 86-26463)

Shaw, D. G. (1984). The effects of learning to program a computer in Basic or Logo on the problem solving abilities of fifth grade students. *Dissertation Abstracts International,* 45(7), 1985A. (University Microfilms No. 84-23897)

Summerville, L. J. (1984). The relationship between computer-assisted instruction and achievement levels and learning rates of secondary school students in first year chemistry. *Dissertation Abstracts International,* 46(3), 603A. (University Microfilms No. 85-10891)

Taylor, V. Y. (1983). Achievement effects on vocabulary, comprehension, and total reading of college students enrolled in a developmental reading program using the drill and practice mode of CAI. *Dissertation Abstracts International,* 44 (8), 2347A. (University Microfilms No. 83-28328)

Todd, W. E. (1986). Effects of computer-assisted instruction on attitudes and achievement of fourth grade students in reading and mathematics. *Dissertation Abstracts International,* 46(11), 3249A. (University Microfilms No. 85-27393)

Turner, L. G. (1986). An evaluation of the effects of paired learning in a mathematics computer-assisted instruction program. *Dissertation Abstracts International,* 46(12), 3641A. (University Microfilms No. 86-02860)

Wainwright, C. L. (1985). The effectiveness of a computer-assisted instruction package in supplementing teaching of selected concepts in high school chemistry: Writing formulas and balancing chemical equations. *Dissertation Abstracts International,* 45(8), 2473. (University Microfilms No. 84-24757)

Ward, P. L. (1986). A comparison of computer-assisted and traditional drill and practice on elementary students' vocabulary knowledge and attitude toward reading instruction. *Dissertation Abstracts International,* 47(8), 2977A. (University Microfilms No. 86-26467)

Wetzel, K. A. (1985). The effect of using a computer in a process writing program on the writing of third, fourth, and fifth grade pupils. *Dissertation Abstracts International,* 47(01), 76. (University Microfilms No.86-85868)

Williams, G. L. (1985). The effectiveness of computer-assisted instruction and its relationship to selected learning-style elements. *Dissertation Abstracts International,* 45(7), 1986A. (University Microfilms No. 84-23909)

REFERENCES:
Miscellaneous Studies

American Psychological Association. (1983). *Publication manual of the American Psychological Association* (3rd ed.). Washington, DC: The Association.

Anderson, R. E., Klassen, D. L., Hansen, T. P., & Johnson, D. C. (1981). The affective and cognitive effects of microcomputer based science instruction. *Journal of Educational Technology Systems*, 9(4), 329-355.

Bangert-Drowns, R. L. (1986). Review of developments in meta-analytic method. *Psychological Bulletin*, 99, 388-399.

Becker, H. J. (1987). *The impact of computer use on children's learning: What research has shown and what it has not.* Baltimore, MD: The Johns Hopkins University.

Bloom, B. S. (1984). The two-sigma problem: The search for methods of group instruction as effective as one-to-one tutoring. *Educational Researcher*, 13(6), 4-16.

Campbell, D. T., & Stanley, J. C. (1963). *Experimental and quasi-experimental designs for research.* Chicago: Rand McNally College Publishing Co.

Clark, R. E. (1983). Reconsidering research on learning from media. *Review of Educational Research*, 53(4), 445-459.

Clark, R. E. (1985). Evidence for confounding in computer-based instruction studies: Analyzing the meta-analyses. *Educational Communication and Technology Journal*, 33(4), 249-262.

Clarke, V. A. (1985/86, Winter). The impact of computers on mathematics abilities and attitudes: A pilot study using Logo. *Journal of Computers in Mathematics and Science Teaching*, pp. 32-33.

Cohen, P. A. (1981, April). *Educational outcomes of tutoring: A meta-analysis of research findings.* Paper presented at the meeting of the American Educational Research Association, Los Angeles, CA.

Collis, B. (1985). Sex differences in secondary school students' attitudes toward computers. *The Computing Teacher*, 12(7), 33-36.

D'Onofrio, M. J., & Slama, M. E. (1985, April). *Negative attitudes toward the subject: A potential impact of using microcomputers to teach traditional courses.* Paper presented at the annual meeting of the American Educational Research Association, Chicago, IL.

Daiute, C., & Kruidenier, J. (1985). A self-questioning strategy to increase young writers' revising processes. *Applied Psycholinguistics*, 6, 307-318.

145

REFERENCES: Miscellaneous Studies (continued)

Dalton, D. W. (1986). A comparison of the effects of Logo and problem-solving strategy instruction on learner achievement, attitude, and problem-solving skills. *Dissertation Abstracts International*, 47(2), 511A. (University Microfilms No. 86-08596)

Dalton, D. W., & Hannafin, M. J. (1986, January). *The effects of video-only, CAI-only, and interactive video instructional systems on learner performance and attitude: An exploratory study.* Paper presented at the annual convention of the Association for Educational Communications and Technology, Las Vegas, NV. (ERIC Document Reproduction Service No. ED 267 762)

Ebeling, B. J. (1981, April). *A meta-analysis of programmed instruction in grades 7-12.* Paper presented at the meeting of the American Educational Research Assocation, Los Angeles, CA.

Eisenberg, Y. (1986, April). The effects of computer-based instruction on college students' interest and achievement. *Educational Technology*, 26, 40-43.

Furor erupts over study's verdict on micros. (April/May, 1987). *School Tech News*, 4 (5), 1.

Fuson, K. C., & Brinko, K. T. (1985). The comparative effectiveness of microcomputers and flash cards in the drill and practice of basic mathematics facts. *Journal for Research in Mathematics Education*, 16(3), 225-232.

Futrell, M. H. (1986). Restructuring teaching: A call for research. *Educational Researcher*, 15(10), 5-8.

Glass, G. V, McGaw, B., & Smith, M. L. (1981). *Meta-analysis in social research.* Beverly Hills, CA: Sage.

Griswold, P. A. (1984). Elementary students' attitudes during 2 years of computer-assisted instruction. *American Educational Research Journal*, 21(4), 737-754.

Harris, J. (1985). Student writers and word processing: A preliminary evaluation. *College Composition and Communication*, 36(3), 323-330.

Hartley, S. S. (1977). Meta-analysis of the effects of individually paced instruction in mathematics. *Dissertation Abstracts International*, 38, 4003A. (University Microfilms No. 77-29926)

Hawkins, J., & Pea, R. D. (1987). Tools for bridging the cultures of everyday and scientific thinking. *Journal of Research in Science Teaching*, 24(4), 291-307.

Hedges, L. V., & Olkin, I. (1985). *Statistical methods for meta-analysis.* Orlando, FL: Academic Press, Inc.

Hedlund, D. E., & Casolara, W. M. (1986, March). Student reactions to the use of computerized experiments in introductory psychology. *Educational Technology*, 26, 42-45.

Hunter, J. E., Schmidt, F. L., & Jackson, G. B. (1983). *Meta-analysis: Cumulating research findings across studies.* Beverly Hills, CA: Sage.

Johnson, J. E. (1985). Characteristics of preschoolers interested in microcomputers.

REFERENCES: Miscellaneous Studies (continued)

Journal of Educational Research, 78(5), 299-305.

Johnson, R. T., Johnson, D. W., & Stanne, M. B. (1986). Comparison of computer-assisted cooperative, competitive, and individualistic learning. *American Educational Research Journal*, 23(3), 382-392.

Jones, M. (1978). *TICCIT applications in higher education: Evaluation results.* Paper presented to the Association for the Development of Computer-Based Instructional Systems, Dallas, TX. (ERIC Document Reproduction Service No. ED 165 706)

Jones, P. K. (1987). The relative effectiveness of computer-assisted remediation with male and female students. *T. H. E. Journal*, 14(7), 61-63.

Kerlinger, F. (1973). *Foundations of behavioral research.* New York: Holt, Rinehart and Winston.

Kulik, J. A. (1985, April). *Consistencies in findings on computer-based education.* Paper presented at the annual meeting of the American Educational Research Association, Chicago, IL.

Kulik, J. A., & Bangert-Drowns, R. L. (1983-84). Effectiveness of technology in precollege mathematics and science teaching. *Journal of Educational Technology Systems*, 12(2), 137-158.

Kulik, J. A., & Kulik, C. C. (1986). *Operative and interpretable effect sizes in meta-analysis.* Paper presented at the meeting of the American Educational Research Association, San Francisco, CA.

Kulik, J. A., & Kulik, C. C. (1987). Review of recent research literature on computer-based instruction. *Contemporary Educational Psychology*, 12, 222-230.

Levin, H. M. (1985). Costs and cost-effectiveness of computer-assisted instruction. *Public Budgeting & Finance*, 5(1), 27-42.

Levin, H. M., Glass, G. V, & Meister, G. (1986). The political arithmetic of cost-effectiveness analysis. *Phi Delta Kappan*, 68, 69-72.

Levin, H. M., & Meister, G. (1986). Is CAI cost-effective? *Phi Delta Kappan*, 67, 745-749.

Louie, S. (1985). *Locus of control among computer-using school children: A report of a pilot study.* Tucson, AZ: National Advisory Council for Computer Implementation in Schools. (ERIC Document Reproduction Service No. ED 260 692)

Loyd, B. H., & Gressard, C. (1984, Winter). The effects of sex, age, and computer experience on computer attitudes. *AEDS Journal*, pp. 67-77.

Lysiak, F., Wallace, S., & Evans, C. (1976). *Computer assisted instruction 1975-76 evaluation report.* Fort Worth: Fort Worth Independent School District. (ERIC Document Reproduction Service No. ED 140 495)

Menis, Y. (1984, May). Improvement in student attitudes and development of scientific curiosity by means of computer studies. *Educational Technology*, pp. 31-32.

Niemiec, R. P., Blackwell, M. C., & Walberg, H. J. (1986). CAI can be doubly effective. *Phi Delta Kappan*, 67, 750-751.

REFERENCES: Miscellaneous Studies (continued)

Papert, S. (1980). *Mindstorms*. New York: Basic Books.

Papert, S. (1987, January-February). Computer criticism vs. technocentric thinking. *Educational Researcher*, 16(1), 22-30.

Pea, R. D. (1983). *Logo programming and problem solving* (Technical Report No. 12). New York: Bank Street College of Education, Center for Children and Technology.

Pea, R. D. (1987, June-July). The aims of software criticism: Reply to Professor Papert. *Educational Researcher*, 16(5), 4-8.

Pea, R. D., & Kurland, D. M. (1984, December). *Toward cognitive technologies for writing* (Technical Report No. 30). New York: Bank Street College of Education, Center for Children and Technology.

Ragosta, M., Holland, P. W., & Jamison, D. T. (1982). *Computer-assisted instruction and compensatory education: The ETS/LAUSD study*. Princeton, NJ: Educational Testing Service.

Roblyer, M. D. (1985b). The greening of educational computing: A proposal for a more research-based approach to computers in instruction. *Educational Technology*, 25(1), 40-44.

Roblyer, M. D., & Castine, W. H. (1987). Instructional computing project uses 'multiplier effect' to train Florida teachers. *T. H. E. Journal*, 14(6), 63-67.

Rosegrant, T. J. (1984). Fostering progress in literacy development: Technology and social interaction. *Seminars in Speech and Language*, 5(1), 47-57.

Rosegrant, T. J. (1985, April). *Using a microcomputer to assist children in their efforts to acquire beginning literacy*. Paper presented at the annual meeting of the American Educational Research Association, Chicago, IL.

Rosegrant, T. J. (1986, April). *It doesn't sound right: The role of speech output as a primary form of feedback for beginning text revision*. Paper presented at the annual meeting of the American Educational Research Association, San Francisco, CA.

Rubin, A., & Bruce, B. (1984, February). *Quill: Reading and writing with a microcomputer* (Reading Education Report No. 48). Cambridge, MA: Bolt Beranek and Newman Inc.

Seymour, S. L., Sullivan, H. J., Story, N. O., & Mosley, M. L. (1986, January). *Microcomputers and continuing motivation*. Paper presented at the annual convention of the Association for Educational Communications and Technology, Las Vegas, NV.

Siann, G., & Macleod, H. (1986). Computers and children of primary school age: Issues and questions. *British Journal of Educational Technology*, 17(2), 133-144.

Slavin, R. E. (1984). Meta-analysis in education: How has it been used? *Educational Researcher*, 13(8), 6-15.

Slavin, R. E. (1986). Best-evidence synthesis: An alternative to meta-analytic and traditional reviews. *Educational Researcher*, 15(9), 5-11.

REFERENCES: Miscellaneous Studies (continued)

Slavin, R. E. (1987). Best-evidence synthesis: Why less is more. *Educational Researcher*, 16(4), 15-16.

Smith, C. L. (1984-85). Relationship of microcomputer-based instruction and learning style. *Journal of Educational Technology Systems*, 13(4), 265-270.

Smith, M. L. (1980). Publication bias and meta-analysis. *Evaluation in Education: An International Review Series*, 4(1), 22-24.

Stebbins, L. B., St.Pierre, R. G., Proper, E. C., Anderson, R. B., & Cerva, T. R. (1977, April). *Education as experimentation: A planned variation model* (An evaluation of Follow Through). Cambridge, MA: ABT Associates Inc.

Suppes, P., & Morningstar, M. (1972). *Computer-assisted instruction at Stanford, 1966-68: Data, models, and evaluation of the arithmetic programs.* New York: Academic Press.

Swadener, M., & Hannafin, M. (1987, January). Gender similarities and differences in sixth graders' attitudes toward computers: An exploratory study. *Educational Technology*, 27, 37-42.

Tallmadge, G. K. (1977). *The Joint Dissemination Review Panel ideabook.* Washington, DC: U. S. Department of Health, Education and Welfare.

Walker, D. F. (1987, June-July). Logo needs research: A response to Papert's paper. *Educational Researcher*, 16(5), 9-11.

Webb, N. M. (1984). Microcomputer learning in small groups: Cognitive requirements and group processes. *Journal of Educational Psychology*, 76(6), 1076-1088.

Zuk, D. (1986). The effects of microcomputers on children's attention to reading. *Computers in the Schools*, 3(2), 39-51.